BRIGHT NOTES

THE IDYLLS OF THE KING AND OTHER POEMS BY ALFRED TENNYSON

Intelligent Education

Nashville, Tennessee

BRIGHT NOTES: The Idylls of the King and Other Poems
www.BrightNotes.com

No part of this publication may be used or reproduced in any manner whatsoever without written permission, except in the case of brief quotations in critical articles and reviews. For permissions, contact Influence Publishers http://www.influencepublishers.com.

ISBN: 978-1-645420-14-9 (Paperback)
ISBN: 978-1-645420-15-6 (eBook)

Published in accordance with the U.S. Copyright Office Orphan Works and Mass Digitization report of the register of copyrights, June 2015.

Originally published by Monarch Press.
David Madison Rogers, 1963
2020 Edition published by Influence Publishers.

Interior design by Lapiz Digital Services. Cover Design by Thinkpen Designs.

Printed in the United States of America.

Library of Congress Cataloging-in-Publication Data forthcoming.
Names: Intelligent Education
Title: BRIGHT NOTES: The Idylls of the King and Other Poems
Subject: STU004000 STUDY AIDS / Book Notes

CONTENTS

1)	Introduction to Alfred Tennyson	1
2)	Introduction to The Idylls of the King	9
3)	The Marriage of Geraint	13
4)	Geraint and Enid	21
5)	Merlin and Vivien	28
6)	Lancelot and Elaine	35
7)	Guinevere	43
8)	The Coming of Arthur	50
9)	The Holy Grail	58
10)	Pelleas and Ettarre	67
11)	The Passing of Arthur	73
12)	The Last Tournament	80

13)	Gareth and Lynette	87
14)	Balin and Balan	94
15)	The Palace of Art	101
16)	In Memoriam	111
17)	Ulysses and Tithonus	130
18)	Lucretius	140
19)	Demeter and Persephone	147
20)	Conclusion	154
21)	Bibliography	159

ALFRED TENNYSON

INTRODUCTION

FAMILY BACKGROUND

Alfred Tennyson was born on August 6, 1809 in his father's rectory at Somersby, the second of eleven surviving children. Tennyson's father, George, had been forced to become a clergyman when he was disinherited from the family fortune in favor of his younger brother. This misfortune had made George Tennyson a gloomy, bitter man, and it cast an oppressive shadow over the crowded little rectory. Despite the gentle sensitivity of his devout mother, Alfred Tennyson bore throughout his life the melancholy disposition inherited from his father and deepened by a long, close association with him. George Tennyson contributed other elements to the development of his son's talent than that of romantic gloom, for he was both a scholar and a book-lover. Tennyson early took full advantage of his father's library and scholarship, and later in life revealed a passion for learning and an accuracy of observation which no doubt reflected the influence of his father.

CHILDHOOD

Like the romantic poets of the previous generation, Tennyson enjoyed an outdoor country life from his earliest days. His companions were his many brothers and sisters and the farm folk living near his home. He did not occupy himself entirely in play, however, for later we find him remarking that his own poems written in early childhood entertained him more than those of other people. The influence of a literary father made itself felt in the precocious childhood verses of Alfred and some of his brothers.

EARLY EDUCATION

From the age of eight until he was twelve, Tennyson attended boarding school at Louth, ten miles from Somersby. Here he was desperately unhappy. The master bullied him and he was not a success with the other boys because he hated games. This experience confirmed him in his love of home and the quiet family circle, as well as in his shyness and suspicion of outsiders, qualities which were to be part of his character throughout his life. After his years at Louth, he was taught by the village schoolmaster for a time, but George Tennyson took increasingly direct charge of his son's education. Under an academic regime that was more comprehensive than methodical, Tennyson flourished as he had not at school. His father's wide-ranging intellect and taste in books afforded young Tennyson a broad classical education without limiting him to the ancient classics. Tennyson was an apt pupil, both at translating classical poetry and at imitating it in original verses of his own. His education was supplemented by the company of his thoughtful and creative brothers, with whom he enjoyed long country walks and literary conversations. The poetry of this adolescent period is marked by contrasting views of nature, which is seen as both tame and wild. Such an idea of nature reflects both the charm of his immediate surroundings and the sensitive, gloomy, chaotic landscape within his own mind.

LIFE AT CAMBRIDGE

Tennyson's attendance at Cambridge rather than Oxford had a great influence upon his future. At Oxford, he would inevitably have been swept up in the "Oxford Movement," which combined a traditional view of religion and the church with excellence in the classics. Cambridge, on the other hand, looked to the future rather than the past, and encouraged an intellectual attitude toward religion, taking account of nineteenth century developments in science. The circle into which Tennyson was drawn, called the "Apostles," was a reform-minded undergraduate society interested in both intellectual and social problems. From the "Apostles" Tennyson drew a sense of his own destiny and his prophetic mission to enlighten his countrymen. The "Apostles" rescued Tennyson from a lonely, unhappy existence in his first months at college. Though his brother Frederick was already at Cambridge, Tennyson found it hard to make friends when he first arrived in 1828. It was common to see his tall, swarthy, fierce-eyed form striding about the campus in lonely grandeur. People remarked even at this period in his life that he had the appearance of a poet, and indeed he enjoyed a small reputation as the joint author, with his brother Frederick, of a modest volume called "Poems by Two Brothers," published at Louth in 1827. After three years, Tennyson left Cambridge without taking a degree.

EARLY CAREER

The friends Tennyson made at Cambridge, among them Arthur Hallam, were tireless admirers of his poetry. They considered him the spokesman of the "Apostles," and the bearer of their message of progress and literary renewal. They gave Tennyson's *Poems, Chiefly Lyrical* (1830) uncritical praise. The volume was gently criticized and mildly approved by a few established critics, who were less sensitive to young Tennyson's genius than his friends were. Tennyson was deeply upset by criticism even later in his career when he was a well-known poet, but in his youth he was particularly vulnerable to critical barbs. Neither Samuel T. Coleridge nor William Wordsworth, both poets whom Tennyson admired and learned from, found much to appreciate in the young poet. Christopher North, an acid-penned critic for the influential *Blackwood* magazine, mixed heavy criticism with a few scant words of praise. In revenge, Tennyson published a little poem ridiculing North in his third volume, put out in 1832. This was an error, for it set North and some of North's friends against the young poet. Many prominent critics agreed that Tennyson was affected and slight, perhaps because of his undeserved reputation as a political radical. Their condemnation of his book was echoed all over England. In his humiliation, Tennyson even considered a self-imposed exile from his country. In his personal life also, Tennyson was plagued by troubles. His dearest friend, the gifted and charming Arthur Hallam, died suddenly in 1833 at the age of twenty-two years. Tennyson's life was shattered by these events and he did not publish anything again for ten years. This was for him a period of emotional crisis, involving the resolution of religious doubts and temptations to despair, as well as a period of creative activity and growth.

ESTABLISHMENT OF REPUTATION

During the period of the "ten years' silence," Tennyson laid the groundwork for the future acceptance of his work. Critics had urged him to write less emotional, lyrical poetry and more of the instructional, homely type demanded by the age. Tennyson wanted to be accepted by his public, and in the poetry published after 1840, he made it clear that he would take the critics' advice. This time his rise and fall were not to be meteoric as it had been between 1828 and 1832, but like the slow, steady advance of the moon across the sky. Not until after the end of Tennyson's long life was his work to suffer critical eclipse again. In 1833, Tennyson retired to his "darling room" at Somersby, where he managed to find ample solitude for work despite the size of his mother's large family. At the rectory, he applied himself to a regime of study that included German, philosophy and science. He may well have determined that no critic would ever again dismiss him as an intellectual lightweight, and he certainly had long since resolved to be a teacher to his generation. Apart from study, his time was profitably spent in the revision of the old, much-criticized poems and the composition of new works, particularly "Ulysses" and "In Memoriam." Soon after Tennyson had left Cambridge, both his father and his grandfather died. The latter, especially, had wanted Tennyson to enter the service of the church. The young man had held both of them off, having no desire to be a clergyman. With their deaths, he was able to follow his own inclination without interference. He became head of the family and took charge of moving them from Somersby to Epping when the new rector took over at their old home.

In the new suburban environment, Tennyson was able to enjoy London society whenever he chose to. Epping proved uncomfortable and not rural enough to please the Tennysons, so they began a series of moves. Despite his grief and introspection, Tennyson was able to socialize in London on occasion. There he was part of a "poets' circle" that included Leigh Hunt, Samuel Rogers, Charles Dickens, William Thackeray, Thomas Carlyle and Walter Savage Landor. Tennyson found a close friend in Carlyle, though their friendship was not based on Carlyle's interest in Tennyson's poetry. Tennyson needed the consolations of friendship, for until his marriage, when he was forty-one, he suffered from frequent depression, due to poverty, ill-health and increasing nearsightedness. He lost what little money he and his family had through a foolish investment, and this disaster was followed by a nervous breakdown. At this point, his friends were able to get him a pension of 200 pounds a year from Sir Robert Peel. His poetic reputation was again on the upswing. In 1835, John Stuart Mill had favorably reviewed the 1832 volume; and by 1837, some reviewers even claimed that Elizabeth Barrett was copying Tennyson's style. Tennyson broke his silence in 1842 by the publication of *Locksley Hall* and *Morte d'Arthur*, which were received kindly by the critics and enthusiastically by the public. These were followed by *The Princess*, a work much admired by the Pre-Raphaelites, a group whose disgust with the squalor of modern England led them to return to the artistic and literary standards in force before the Renaissance.

FARRINGFORD PERIOD

Peel's grant of a pension and his promising prospects as a poet allowed Tennyson to marry Emily Sellwood in 1850, after an engagement of fourteen years. This gentle woman largely succeeded in domesticating the gloomy poet, and some critics have held her responsible for the increasingly affected and sentimental elements in much of his poetry. His love for solitude kept Tennyson from mingling frequently with intellectuals and literary men from whom he might have gained new insights and received healthy criticism. Emily gave him the security of love and approval; she served as a capable and devoted secretary but could not serve effectively as a literary critic. The publication of "In Memoriam" (1850) and the approval it won from Queen Victoria and her consort led to Tennyson's being offered the Laureateship in 1850. As **Poet Laureate**, he was subject to the rigors of fame, and when he retired with Emily to Farringford, on the Isle of Wight, she had to shield him from curious intruders so that he could work. The public, like Queen Victoria, loved "In Memoriam," so the critics had to revise their initial unfavorable comments about the work. In March of 1862, Tennyson was summoned by the Queen to visit her at Osborne, her home on the Isle of Wight. The visit began a warm friendship which developed primarily through letters and ended only with the poet's death.

ALDWORTH PERIOD

Tennyson found the tourists at Farringford too annoying, so he built a house at Haslemere in Surrey, called Aldworth. Despite its relative isolation, tourists followed him there also, and with them came distinguished Victorian personages. Tennyson's home was now becoming a national shrine, embodying in its atmosphere all the virtues which Victorians honored and believed themselves to possess. Roses were named after him; his opinions on all subjects were eagerly solicited and accepted by all Englishmen. The public pressure on Tennyson's personal life became ever stronger, and in 1874 Emily's health broke under the strain of serving as both housewife and secretary. Their son, Hallam, had to be recalled from Cambridge to serve his father as secretary in his mother's place. Tennyson had to be protected from any unflattering reviews, which he was still too sensitive to bear. He was also averse to biographies, as he was to all efforts of the public to relate the poet's life to his poetry. His son Hallam was entrusted with the mission to report his father's life accurately in order to forestall the prying of others. Despite his hatred of criticism, Tennyson was considered by those who knew him well as a straightforward, modest man, who was incapable of intellectual or artistic pretense. This judgment must be weighed against the common belief that Tennyson was overly anxious to please his complacent Victorian audience, and to suppress his inferior early work.

LAST YEARS

In old age, Tennyson was nearly as vigorous as he was in youth. His volumes of poetry followed one another in rapid succession, the last being published three weeks after his death. The conclusion to Tennyson's life was one of mingled sorrows and triumphs. In 1884 he reluctantly accepted a peerage from his old friend, Prime Minister Gladstone, which he considered as much an honor to literature as to himself. His son Lionel died at sea of a fever in 1886, and the grieving father commemorated his son's passing in *Demeter and Other Poems*. Tennyson was, in his last years, often overwhelmed by a sense of futility, perhaps because he had aimed so high. His *Idylls of the King* had been meant to instruct Englishmen in the high ideals of nobility and chivalry, but it seemed to him that the world honored these ideals less and less. After a brief period of declining health, Tennyson died peacefully, surrounded by his family, the moonlit silence of his room broken only by the words of his own prayer on the lips of a friend. He had dominated the poetic scene of England for sixty years and had been the voice of his age's struggle for serenity and faith.

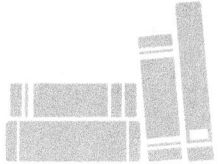

THE IDYLLS OF THE KING

INTRODUCTION

COMPOSITION

Tennyson had considered writing an **epic** on the subject of Arthur early in his poetic career. The *Lady of Shalott* (1833), his first treatment of the Elaine story, was written the year of his friend Hallam's death. Having idealized Arthur Hallam in a personal way in "In Memoriam," Tennyson was later to carry this identification into a larger, less restricted allegorical figure, that of the mythical King Arthur. In his *Memoir*, Tennyson said of the *Idylls*: "It is not the history of one man or of one generation, but a whole cycle of generations." The fragment *Morte d'Arthur* was written in 1835, and in a volume published in 1842 the ballads *Sir Lancelot and Queen Guinevere*, and *Sir Galahad* appeared. The series of idylls that were ultimately to be gathered into one organized, thematically united whole was not seriously begun until 1856. The final touches were not applied to the work until 1885, so that the poet spread his Arthurian labors over nearly half a century. Critics have said that the *Idylls* lack perfect unity of technique and **theme**, but one of the most remarkable features of the work is that Tennyson managed to maintain the high level of continuity and style that he did, over the extensive period of composition.

DATES

The first four idylls to be published were "Enid," "Vivien," "Elaine" and "Guinevere" (1859), which were paired as studies in feminine opposites. Ten years later the volume appeared which contained "The Coming of Arthur," "The Holy Grail," "Pelleas and Ettarre" and "The Passing of Arthur." "The Last Tournament" and "Gareth and Lynette" were published in 1871 and 1872, respectively, and the Enid story was divided into two parts in 1872. This was done to bring the number of idylls up to twelve, presumably so that the symbolic year would be completely represented. "Balin and Balan," though written fifteen years earlier, was not published until 1885.

SOURCES

Interest in the Middle Ages had been stimulated by the Romantic poets of the early nineteenth century, as well as by the Gothic architectural revival and the writings of Ruskin and the Tractarians of Oxford. With the revival of the medieval period in the imagination of nineteenth century England came an upsurge of interest in the Arthurian story. This body of legendary material centering on a possibly genuine fifth century Anglo-Roman leader, Arturius, was to English popular lore what Siegfried was to the Germans and The Cid was to the Spanish. The chronicle of Nennius (in which the Arthurian story first appears) is usually dated c. 800 A. D., but may be as early as the sixth century. It places Arthur as a local hero who defended the civilized population against the invading Saxons when the

Romans retreated from Northern England just beyond the River Humber. The legend was expanded in the *History of the Kings of Britain* by Geoffrey of Monmouth (c. 1150), in which the symbolic and miraculous aspects of the familiar Arthurian story begin to appear, as well as resemblances to the life of Christ. Other authors throughout the Middle Ages and early modern period developed the Arthurian materials; and the greatest and most influential of these was Sir Thomas Malory, whose loose collection of tales, *Morte d'Arthur* (c. 1470), was the primary source for Alfred Tennyson. Edmund Spenser's *Faerie Queen* (1589-96) also treated the Arthurian legend, and the Arthur pictured in this work is an idealized, Christ-like figure like Tennyson's Arthur, much different from the human and imperfect Arthur of Malory. Although Tennyson used some of Malory's humanizing techniques, it was to the holy and heroic King Arthur of the ancient chronicles that he returned for his inspiration.

STYLE AND STRUCTURE

The word "idyll" is from the Greek, and means a brief picture, scene or sketch; usually it refers to a poem of rural life. Tennyson used the idyll as a sketch, but not as a rural one. His Arthurian poems fell into the idyll category not because of their subject, but because of their self-contained narrative and impressionistic description. Tennyson excelled in creating an atmosphere and in communicating the moods and feelings of characters; but he did not have the "narrative gift," or that lively, dramatic quality which marks the good novelist. Instead of constructing his **blank verse epic** in the Greek style, with events proceeding chronologically in an orderly fashion, Tennyson saw the action of the poems as an eternal moment, as though with the eye of God. Events are looked back upon or forward to, and seen in relation to the whole pattern. Often an idyll begins with a short passage that belongs to the middle or end of the story in terms of action. Individual scenes are chosen for treatment in depth, with special emphasis on their descriptive possibilities, rather than on the logical advancement of the "story line." The poet then uses the flashback to illuminate the initial passage.

While the structure of individual idylls varies, there is a single pattern detectable in the twelve poems as a whole, which is similar to the three acts of a play. In each "act" there are three poems, reflecting the dominant mood of the beginning, middle and final aspects of the cycle. The first act pictures the establishment of the Arthurian order. The menace of the waste land is introduced, but only in a whisper; obstacles to virtue are within the characters themselves and are overcome by the virtues of other characters. In Act II the danger to the Round Table and its ideals becomes obvious. The innocent Elaine comes to grief, and the asceticism of the most gallant knights leads to a removal of them from the real world where Arthur needs them to battle against Britain's enemies. The **theme** of Act III is the perversion of the ideal and the resulting destruction of Arthur's order. The goal of Pelleas and Tristram is a worldly one: profane love. "The Last Tournament" is won by the champion of cynicism and evil conduct. At the end, the cycle is seen in its eternal significance, so that Arthur's virtue and accomplishment are revealed as meaningful for the ultimate destiny of man, even though the forces of death and disintegration seem to have carried the day. Tennyson insists that reality is more than it seems to the senses, and that it must be sought in the eternal, spiritual vision of man in his journey toward God.

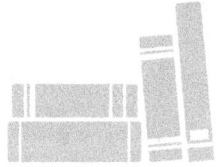

THE IDYLLS OF THE KING

THE MARRIAGE OF GERAINT

PLOT ANALYSIS

Geraint, Prince of Devon and Arthur's knight, enjoyed a perfect marriage with the beautiful Enid, until Enid's close friendship with Queen Guinevere began to disturb Geraint. There were rumors that Guinevere loved Lancelot and not Arthur, and Geraint feared that the taint of her friend's fault might soil Enid's character. To prevent this, he told Arthur that he needed to pacify his own princedom, and took Enid from the court.

Enid worried that people talked of Geraint's loss of manhood because he spent too much time isolated with her in their castle. One night, Geraint awoke to hear Enid murmuring in tears that she was "no true wife." In a jealous rage, Geraint ordered her to wear the old dress she had worn when he met her, and ride before him in silence upon a quest. The dress made Enid recall their meeting and marriage in the previous year.

That adventure had begun with Arthur leaving on a hunt for a mysterious white hart, which the queen had been too languorous to follow with the others. While Guinevere dallied behind, dreaming of Lancelot, Geraint joined her. They encountered a strange knight, accompanied by his lady and a dwarf. When Guinevere sent first her maiden and then Geraint to ask after the knight's identity, both her messengers were struck by the whip of the insolent dwarf. Unarmed, Geraint followed the trio, determined to track them to their home. He planned to borrow arms and avenge the insult to the queen.

Geraint arrived at the knight's fortress, only to learn that the tournament of the sparrow-hawk was to be held the next day, and that neither arms nor lodging was to be had in the area, except at the house of the old, dispossessed Earl Yniol. Geraint found the old man, his wife, and their beautiful daughter, Enid, living in a ruined castle, though they had once ruled the earldom. Yniol told Geraint that Enid had refused to marry the proud Knight of the Sparrow-hawk, who was Yniol's nephew, as she had refused the drunken Limours before him. In revenge, the Sparrow-hawk had seized and sacked their castle and usurped the earldom. Each year he defeated all challengers at a tournament, with a prize of a golden sparrow-hawk for the winner to give his lady. Yniol informed Geraint that without a lady whom he considered the fairest in the world, he could not win, and Geraint eagerly declared his love for Enid.

Using Yniol's ancient, rusted arms, Geraint appeared at the tournament. Seeing Enid and recalling the insult to Guinevere, Geraint was possessed by such strength that he overthrew the proud, well-armed Knight of the Sparrow-hawk, and made him admit his name: Edyrn, son of Nudd. Edyrn was made to go back to Arthur's court and make his apologies, as well as to surrender Yniol's earldom to its rightful owner. Having done these things, Edyrn reformed and entered Arthur's service. Enid, who was to accompany Geraint back to Arthur's court (then Caerleon on the Usk), feared to disgrace her betrothed by her poor attire.

Her mother presented her with the beautiful gown that had been stolen from her when Edyrn had sacked their castle, and Enid was delighted that the gown of which she had dreamed was again hers. But when Geraint heard of the gown from Yniol, he ordered Enid to change back into her old dress. He desired to have her clothed by Queen Guinevere, who had promised to adorn his bride and be her friend. Obediently, Enid put on the old dress, just as she did a year later when distrust had sprung up between her and her husband.

CHARACTER ANALYSES

Geraint

A man who is violent and single-minded in his passions and in his virtues, Geraint is often blinded by those very qualities that make him great. When he considers Guinevere virtuous, he spares no pains to compliment her, to join her in friendship to his Enid and to hasten off to avenge her honor without even procuring weapons first. When he has one suspicion of Guinevere's fault, he whisks Enid off to the country, abandons Arthur and ruins his own warlike reputation. At a few misconstrued words from his noble wife, whom he had vowed always to trust, Geraint takes extreme measures to test her fidelity.

Enid

A type of the perfect servant like Gareth, Enid has none of the faults that mark an ordinary individual's personality. She is absolutely obedient to her superiors. She serves her father, even as a cook and cleaning woman, and serves guests as keeper of their horses. When she marries, she serves Geraint in the same way, when he demands it. She is always more concerned for his honor than for her own happiness, and is eager for him to redeem his good name. Like the perfect wife she is, however, she holds his safety above all else, even obedience, and in Geraint, she proves that such loving disobedience is the essence of fidelity.

Yniol

Like his daughter Enid, Yniol is perfectly resigned in the face of disaster. His very virtues, gentleness and liberality, cause his ruin, because he cannot be violent in the face of violence. He acknowledges humbly that he sometimes despises himself for being so weak as to have let men live as they pleased, without being a tyrant. Yet he admits that suffering wrongs does not disturb his peace, as long as he himself does not inflict wrongs on others.

Comment

Arthur's court is no longer what it was at first. Guinevere now dreams of another man, and rumors fly about her. Without Guinevere's perfect fidelity, Arthur's mission will inevitably fail. The tragedy now begins to take root and grow at the court. Instead of viewing the effects of mistrust in the life of the queen and the "blameless king," we see it in the marriage of Geraint and Enid. Geraint, as a bold and virtuous knight, is identified with both the sun and with Arthur throughout the poem, and suffers all the tortures of doubt which the king is too exalted to feel.

Throughout the two stories of Geraint, there is a pattern of love's development to maturity. In order to have a love based on truth, the lovers must overcome the world of appearances and know one another in terms of ultimate realities. Early in their marriage, Geraint loves to have Enid dressed in splendid garments, so that he and others may contemplate her beauty. Thus dressed, Enid exists in an artificial world, one into which mistrust and deceit commonly come. When she wore her old dress as a maiden, and when she wears it again in the next tale, during her trial, she proves herself worthy of Geraint's love in the rough atmosphere of the real world. After the initial idyllic and unreal stage of their marriage, Geraint and Enid experience a coming to maturity through the painful reality of suspicion and misunderstanding.

The first awareness that all is not well, even far away from the court, is suggested in Geraint's absorption in attending Enid, and his forgetfulness of manly vows. A marriage based on reality must not betray the destiny of the man, but must help to fulfill it; and Enid, unlike Bellicent, does not wish to keep a man enthralled. From being sunk in domestic joys, Geraint awakes abruptly, stirred to seek again both self-respect and masculine identity. Unlike Arthur, he is destined to succeed because his wife gives him perfect devotion. It is through this devotion that triumph must come for a man, if it is to come at all. In the *Idylls* as a whole, the masculine must be forged with a perfectly dutiful and adoring feminine in order to be creative and constructive in the world of events. Subduing one's lesser nature and the evil always present in the world is symbolized by Gareth's eventual victory over the dwarf who had insulted Guinevere.

There are mythological overtones throughout "The Marriage of Geraint." One is the rescue of the woman by a hero who later marries her, a theme common in Greek myths like that of Perseus and Andromeda. Another mythological element is the constant relation of Geraint to the sun and its power. This identification binds him to Arthur, also a solar hero. Geraint wears a scarf of royal purple, decorated with two golden apples, symbolic both of his heroic superiority to other men and of his likeness to the sun, source of life and power. The sparrow-hawk, an ancient symbol of the sun's strength, was consecrated by the Egyptians, Greeks and Romans to the sun. Geraint made the sun's power his own by winning the sacred emblem.

In many myths, the hero overthrows a ruling king and assumes the defeated king's symbols of power. By forcing the Knight of the Sparrow-hawk to reveal his true identity as Edyrn, Geraint won the right to assume the identity of the sparrow-hawk himself. With that right, he gained Enid, over whom Edyrn had had power in the past.

The third mythological element is the Wheel of Fortune, of which Enid sings when Geraint first sees her. Enid herself is twice cast down by Fortune in the two tales, and ultimately restored to her high position, just as Edyrn is elevated, cast down, and then restored at Arthur's court. Character is tested and revealed by the maintenance of serenity in the face of Fortune's surprises.

ESSAY QUESTIONS AND ANSWERS

Question: How is the sin of pride viewed in the idyll? How does the contrast between Edyrn and Yniol illustrate the fall of the proud?

Answer: In "The Marriage of Geraint," as in life, pride is essentially a sin against reality itself. Anyone who refuses to recognize himself and his condition for what they are, risks falling into the sin of pride. Even Geraint's pride in Enid at first is exaggerated, not because its object is unworthy, but because pride blinds

Geraint to other equally important aspects of his life. It drives him to a false view of reality, because of which he deserts his king and sees imaginary evil in his wife's character. Because he views things with a single-minded, passionate gaze, Geraint unknowingly betrays both his king and his wife. His vision is only corrected by the proof of Enid's character as exhibited in real deeds, for reality itself is an overwhelming corrective for the proud.

Edyrn depends upon outward trappings of power for his happiness and his sense of his own worth. He goes about accompanied by a nasty little dwarf, who is a symbol of Edyrn's own moral inferiority. He cannot see himself for what he is, even when he is rejected by Enid, but commits violent acts against others out of pride in himself and his position. He tries to increase his own stature by decreasing that of everyone around him. As the Sparrow-hawk, symbolic of the sun's power, Edyrn masqueraded in a greatness which he did not truly possess. Only when Geraint's victory in the tournament reveals unmistakably to Edyrn that he is not the great hero he believed himself to be, can Edyrn humble himself before Arthur and win both pardon and a new life. Yniol is not blinded by pride like his nephew, but is gentle and generous in fortune as well as in defeat. He does not change his attitude or his deeds with his fortune, but maintains a single-minded serenity in the face of trouble. In contrast to Edyrn's inability to see himself in true perspective, Yniol's character is marked by clear self-knowledge, of both his own weaknesses and his own virtues.

Question: How does the idea of the hunt figure in the symbolism of "The Marriage of Geraint"?

Answer: The hunt for the white hart, which begins the story of Geraint's adventure, represents the quest for innocence, virtue and justice that characterizes Arthur's mission. It is noteworthy that Guinevere does not rise in the morning for the hunt, but is lost in dreams of Lancelot; her sinful attachment prevents her from that active pursuit of goodness which Arthur's hunt represents. Geraint also does not enter the hunt, but for reasons different from Guinevere's. Arthur's hunt is parallel to his own, which is about to begin. Geraint, however, hunts a man, the Sparrow-hawk, rather than a beast. Ironically, the hawk is also a hunter, a bird of prey. His victim is Enid, who is often compared with a nightingale. The symbol of the hunt allows the outward action of the narrative to coincide with the inward development of Geraint, who is hunting perfection.

THE IDYLLS OF THE KING

GERAINT AND ENID

PLOT ANALYSIS

Enid and Geraint rode out into the wilds of Geraint's princedom. Breaking Geraint's command, Enid warned him of three evil knights waiting in ambush. When he had killed them, he made Enid drive their horses before her. Again they encountered three antagonists, one a giant, against whom Enid warned Geraint. He overthrew these three also, and had Enid drive their horses with the others through the woods. At last they came to a meadow, where a kindly poor boy took pity on the tired Enid and offered the two some food. In return, Geraint gave him a horse and armor, and asked him to get them simple lodging for the night. While they sat in their rented room, not speaking to one another, Enid's old suitor, Limours, came to them and greeted Geraint warmly. Seeing that Enid was unhappy, he approached her and declared his love. Enid pretended interest to prevent him from killing Geraint then and there, and told him to come for her later. When they were alone, she informed Geraint. The two leave suddenly in the night, giving their host five horses and sets of armor for his trouble.

Leaving the district of Earl Limours, they entered that of the robber Earl Doorm. Limours and his men followed them, but when Geraint killed the earl, his men dispersed and left the couple alone. Without telling Enid that he was bleeding from a wound under his armor, Geraint rode proudly on. At last he fell by the side of the road from exhaustion and loss of blood. While Enid sat weeping beside him, Earl Doorm and his band rode by. Because of Enid's beauty, he instructed his men to carry Geraint back to his hall. Geraint lay there for hours, with Enid beside him; even after he awoke, he would not speak to her, so that her fidelity could be tested further.

Doorm returned, and while at the table, he noticed Enid again. He invited her to come and eat beside him, saying that she was the fairest woman he had ever seen and that he would make her his wife. When Enid refused to come, the Earl dragged her to the table, and tried in vain to force her to eat and drink. In a rage, Doorm ordered her to put on a fine robe instead of her poor gown, but Enid refused again, saying she obeyed no one but Geraint. Thinking there was no other way to deal with such a stubborn woman, Doorm struck her lightly on the cheek. At this, Enid cried out, not for pain but because she feared Doorm would not have dared to hit her if Geraint were still alive. Hearing her cry, Geraint leaped from his bed and cut off Doorm's head with one stroke. Doorm's men fled, leaving Geraint to apologize to Enid and promise never to doubt her again.

As the two flee Doorm's hall on Geraint's charger, they met Edyrn, who had been sent by Arthur to warn Doorm of retribution. Edyrn allayed Enid's fears, by explaining that he had amended his former life, and thanking her for her role in his redemption. Having been brought to Arthur by Edyrn, Geraint heard his king praise the converted knight as being greater than one who had done wonders with the sword, because that knight had done violence to the evil within himself. At this, Geraint realized that his exploits were of slight consequence. Arthur had come to Geraint's country to rid it of robbers and evil earls, for he had taken Geraint's absence from the court as a personal reproach. While Geraint recovered from his wound, Arthur put the earldom in order. They all returned together to Caerleon, where Guinevere once again welcomed Enid as her friend. After a brief visit, Enid and Geraint went back to their own castle to raise their family. Geraint's happy life was crowned by death in battle for the king against the heathen.

CHARACTER ANALYSES

Limours

Eaten up by passion and selfishness, Limours is the type of man who can never achieve self-mastery. The prize for which he and all other men in the idyll labor, is Enid, the symbol for fidelity to duty, perfect integrity, and perseverance in the face of adversity. In desiring Enid, Limours desires what is forever beyond him because of his own weakness of character. He is stealthy, accepting Geraint's hospitality while intent upon stealing Geraint's wife. Unlike Geraint, a man of noble action, Limours is merely a crafty man of words. He is witty and charming, able to fool Geraint and those around him into accepting him as a good fellow. He cannot fool the steadfast Enid, however, for she knows him by his deeds and sees behind the mask of amorous, self-pitying words.

Doorm

Though a man who represents all that is wild and ugly in the wasteland outside Arthur's domain, Doorm has distinguishing traits that mark him as a personality in his own right. Although others pass by the weeping Enid and her fallen lord, Doorm was moved to stop and speak to her, albeit roughly. He has an eye for quality, coarse robber though he is, for he is quick to see that Enid is a rare and noble woman, just as he notes that Geraint's charger is a "noble one." He is, however, dominated by the demands of the flesh, and fulfills these by violence. He warns Enid that he will compel her to do his will, and he clearly has no respect for the desires of anyone but himself. Doorm is also a man dominated by appearances. He insists that beauty must "go beautifully," and that without the trappings of beauty, neither love nor loveliness can exist.

Comment

"Geraint and Enid" begins with a brief commentary by the poet on the theme that is common to the poem as a whole, as well as to this particular idyll: the contrast between the world of appearance and that of reality. The dramatic tension throughout the *Idylls* depends on the hero's attempt to realize the ideal (heaven) in terms of the everyday life of human beings on earth. The ideal is the ultimately real, beside which the world of appearances dominating our senses grows shadowy. Arthur manages to balance the ideal and the actual worlds in a precarious relationship during the first third of the *Idylls*, but his difficulties are already apparent. Even within the circle of the Round Table itself, where the ideal is most perfectly fused with the life of men, earthly values begin to corrupt the dedication of men to their spiritual goal. Arthur has men maintain their status as spiritual beings with bodies of clay by urging a life of good works, in which the body is a proper vehicle for the soul. The body is also, in Arthur's world, a weapon for the spirit, not a bad influence upon it that forces the spirit to compromise with ideals.

Geraint, standing in Arthur's place, is called upon to order his ideas of truth and untruth, so that he may make proper use of reality. This does not happen until Geraint, through deeds of love and violence, has deepened and perfected his knowledge of spiritual and earthly reality. Each of the victories requires the assistance of Enid, though Geraint will not admit it until the end, when he has regained his grip on the world as it really is. Ultimately, he must do battle for the sake of Enid, whom he had despised; and in this paradox, he learned the meaning of love, trust and humanity.

The crisis of Geraint's achievement of mastery over himself comes at the point when he dispatches Doorm in mortal combat. The brutal earl is a counterpart of Geraint's baser self. Geraint himself admits after the victory that he had treated Enid worse than Doorm had. Doorm had assaulted Enid with cruel words and a blow, treating her as a possession and not a person. By doubting Enid's good faith and stripping her of home and noble garments, Geraint used her shabbily, not according to her worth. When he kills Doorm, he kills also that evil brute within himself that made him cruel to the one he loved most.

Enid's constancy is the force that works for Geraint's redemption, that is, for his maturing into perfect manhood, just as Enid's purity is the indirect motivation for Edyrn's conversion. At first, Edyrn had desired only revenge against Enid for rejecting him. However, when he is changed at Arthur's court into a man capable of acting according to ideals, Edyrn becomes a loyal and sympathetic friend to Enid and Geraint. He, like Geraint, masters his baser self, and becomes a true disciple of King Arthur. Arthur kisses Enid purely, like a brother, and considerately takes her to her tent when she comes to his camp. His manner toward women, marked by courtesy and protectiveness, is the mark of a man who has achieved heroic stature in both heavenly and earthly terms.

ESSAY QUESTION AND ANSWER

Question: What are the symbols of disorder in the idyll? How is Geraint's quest related to the mission of Arthur to end disorder in his realm?

Answer: Disorder in "Geraint and Enid" is both internal and external. The landscape within the soul of the jealous man, Geraint, of Limours, and of the sensual Doorm, is represented by the robber-infested wilderness through which the couple travels. In the *Idylls* as a whole, Arthur must battle for the souls of men and not merely for their material welfare. It is only when he is betrayed by the hearts of his closest loved ones, Guinevere and Lancelot, that Arthur's realm falls into chaos. Soul and body, spiritual destiny and earthly events, are indissolubly bound together.

The wild horses which Enid is commissioned by Geraint to drive before him represent all those fierce, violent elements in his own character and those of all men, which only the purity and gentleness of woman can harness and guide. As Enid calms and trains the animals, so she helps Geraint to conquer himself. Only when he has overcome his own passions, is Geraint fit to serve Arthur, bringing real manhood to that service. Civil disorder in the *Idylls* is always associated with moral evil or disorder of the soul. Arthur represents the perfect order within the soul, warring nobly with all that is base. The kingdom he desires to establish is one in which serenity of spirit and trust in the word of others contrast with raging, violent passion and doubt of others' good faith.

THE IDYLLS OF THE KING

MERLIN AND VIVIEN

PLOT ANALYSIS

Having heard from a visiting minstrel that Lancelot and other of Arthur's knights had bound themselves to celibacy, Vivien decided, on King Mark's suggestion, to go to Arthur's court and stir up trouble. All was peaceful at the court when Vivien begged to be admitted as a refugee from the unwanted attentions of King Mark. The knights had only jousts and tournaments to occupy them, so that the evil gossip planted everywhere by Vivien had much opportunity to flourish. Because Vivien had tried unsuccessfully to flirt with Arthur, all the knights laughed at her. She was determined to win the heart of old Merlin, the second greatest man at court. Flattered by her attentions, Merlin could not resist encouraging Vivien's friendship.

Melancholy over his sense of impending doom, Merlin sailed with Vivien to Brittany. In the wild forest of Broceliande, by a huge old oak tree, Merlin sat wrapped in thought, while Vivien tried to coax from him the charm which would render a man invisible, insensible and forever imprisoned in a hollow tower. She first attempted to convince Merlin that he should prove his love and trust by confiding in her, but Merlin said he had trusted her too much in telling her even of the charm's existence. To illustrate to Vivien how her wiles distracted him from the purpose of his life, Merlin told her a story.

By the very oak tree near which they sat, Merlin and a dozen or so friends had met to hunt a hart with golden horns. At the same time, talk first arose of establishing the Round Table. One warrior, enflamed, burst into a noble song, so loud that the hart was frightened away, forever lost to the hunters.

Vivien pouted that Merlin kept women locked up in towers with his charm, but Merlin would not take her jealousy seriously. He told her the story of the charm:

A far eastern king seized a beautiful woman from a pirate captain and made her his queen. Because everyone fell victim to her beauty, the king sought a charm which would make her belong to him alone. Many wizards tried and failed to produce such a charm, and were killed for their failure. At last, the king forced a mystical hermit to reveal the charm, and caused the queen to vanish for all men but her husband. The hermit returned to his wilderness, then disappeared. His book, with the charm in it, came into Merlin's hands. The book was written in an ancient language, with microscopic letters; and the charm had been deciphered by Merlin only with the greatest difficulty, in the hermit's marginal comment.

Merlin declared he feared Vivien would use the charm in revenge on some knight of Arthur's court who mocked her, if not on himself. In fury, Vivien poured forth her foul rumors and slanders against Arthur's knights, especially against Lancelot. When Merlin withdrew in disgust, Vivien wept and again pleaded her love for him. She swore an oath that she was no schemer, but was almost struck by a bolt of lightning. In fear, Vivien jumped into Merlin's arms, uttering passionate cries of devotion. As a storm began around them, Merlin embraced her. Warmed by their mutual love, he told her the charm. As he slept afterward, Vivien employed the charm to imprison him in the great oak tree, where he lay insensible forever. Triumphantly, Vivien declared she now possessed Merlin's glory as her own, because she had overcome him.

CHARACTER ANALYSES

Merlin

A wizard among ordinary men, Merlin is one who has mastered all secrets, arts and skills. He is no common mortal, for his blood has "earnest in it of far springs to be," and his knowledge reaches back into time as well as into the future. With such great wisdom, he is able to look upon himself objectively, seeing himself as he really is, and he is also able to see Vivien's character without illusion. Yet his need for human affection is no less, for all his wisdom. He has not desired fame or public adulation, he declares, but his reaction to Vivien indicates that flattery plays a larger part in his life than he cares to admit. He boasts lightly to Vivien that he has never needed charms to win the love of women, half-believing that Vivien really loves him. In his pride, he misjudges the woman he confides in, and thinks she loves him more than she does.

Vivien

When she describes her birth, Vivien makes clear her real nature. Her father died in battle against Arthur, and her mother died upon his corpse after giving birth to Vivien. She views herself as being "born from death," and carrying death and sin wherever she goes. Brought up at the evil court of King Mark, she can believe no one pure, and all her conduct is characterized by a thorough-going cynicism. When she observes the behavior of the knights and ladies at Arthur's court, she always interprets it in the worst light, according to her own base laws of conduct. Vivien's evil is not the result of sudden passion, but coldly calculated and carried out through wily manipulation of people and events.

Comment

At the beginning of the idyll, the minstrel introduces a hint of that duality or disharmony which dominates the rest of the work. Though Arthur has not commanded celibacy, the young knights, in imitation of the lovesick Lancelot, bind themselves to an ideal beyond their strength. The ideal itself is one which cuts men off from that special, healing, reconciling power of the feminine, needed in the world if the ideal is to become reality. This dualism, in which the spirit sunders itself from the flesh, contributes to the downfall of Arthur's hopes, for the flesh overcomes the spirit when the two work against each other. Merlin's fall at the end of the idyll is a logical outcome of the divorce between spirit and body. His wisdom cannot save him from his passion, because he has not fused them in a holy love for a good woman.

Vivien acts as a symbol of that evil which insidiously worms its way into the noblest, purest places, and gradually corrupts them. She herself remarks that evil is a "little rat that borest in the dyke," and proceeds to play that role in the court of Arthur. As the king represents all that is high and virtuous, Vivien represents flesh, cynicism, lechery and death. She spreads the poison of her rumors slowly through the body of the court, so that at last even Arthur is troubled by what he has heard. Her effect on Merlin reveals the nature of evil's attack on a good man. At first he merely tolerates her and laughs at her slanders, but ultimately he comes to depend upon her flattery and protestations of love, even to love her "somewhat." Such a friendship inevitably leaves its mark on Merlin's soul, for toleration of evil and dalliance with it tempt a man to further involvement in sin. As soon as Merlin becomes entangled in Vivien's net, he loses touch with the ideal of Arthur's court. He grows melancholy, convinced that the battle against evil and death is futile. Without uncompromising loyalty of both mind and body to the holy cause, Merlin cannot maintain his faith and virtue. Nor does he love Vivien with a high or holy love. He knows her wickedness, and his love has no illusions. She simply amuses him and offers him diversion in his wearisome old age.

Merlin knows that Vivien is keeping him from his mission. He links her effect upon him with the song of the warrior about the glories of the Round Table, which frightened away the hart with golden horns. The hunt here symbolizes the quest for spiritual and earthly integrity, as it did in "The Marriage of Geraint." As the warriors lost sight of the real goal (the hart) for the sake of an illusory glory (the song), so Merlin allows himself to be distracted from the pursuit of virtuous wisdom by the carnal attractions of Vivien. He tells Vivien that once he advised a young knight to think less of fame and more of being useful to the world. The idea of his mission in life is always in his mind, a redeeming impulse which works against the destructive influence of Vivien. His melancholy stems in part from his awareness that Vivien's presence is a threat to him, and that like a wave she will drown him, his good name and his capacity for righteous action. Vivien represents the devouring woman, contrasting with the complementary feminine ideal (like Enid). The evil type of woman betrays man, wipes out his identity and prevents him from fulfilling his noble destiny. Her victory over Merlin is a disastrous omen for the future of Arthur's mission, which depends upon a woman's fidelity.

ESSAY QUESTIONS AND ANSWERS

Question: How does cynicism contrast with idealism in "Merlin and Vivien"?

Answer: The central portion of the *Idylls* is concerned with the perversion of the ideal, as the first portion is devoted to its establishment and the last to its dissolution. Those who maintain their faith in the ideal grow fewer, and those whose point of view is more or less cynical grow more numerous. Merlin's fall is due to a failure to keep faith with the ideal of his manhood, and that fall is the prelude to the fall of the Round Table itself. Vivien is the representative of the evil at King Mark's court, which has come to corrupt King Arthur; she is also the voice of cynicism, which declares that the ideal cannot exist in the flesh. Vivien believes that power, the only worthwhile goal for man, can be gained through shattering the illusions that bind the idealists to their faith. When virtue has been exposed to all eyes for the phantom she is sure it is, Vivien's triumph and that of the cynical point of view will be complete. Yet Vivien's thesis does not hold true for Arthur. He is too pure even to notice her attempt upon his virtue, and so Arthur remains as a living refutation of those who cannot believe in the true destiny of men: the perfection and transfiguration of human goodness.

Question: What symbols of disorder are present in "Merlin and Vivien"?

Answer: Although Vivien is the chief representative of destructive and disintegrating forces in the idyll, symbols of her mission are scattered throughout the poem. Chief among these is the storm. A storm first brings to King Mark's court the minstrel who reveals the celibate practices at Arthur's court. It is this information which first attracts Vivien to Camelot. Her final evil is accomplished during the storm at Broceliande: the defeat and ruin of Merlin who has been the seer of the king and a major force for good in Arthur's kingdom. Vivien herself is perceived in symbolic form. Merlin dreams of her as a wave, destined to fall and break upon him, destroying him and his mission on earth. The place in which Vivien works her wiles is the wilderness of Broceliande, a type of wasteland like the woods around Camelot. Such places represent disorder and disaster, for they continually threaten the precarious human order built up at the cost of such great effort by Arthur and Merlin.

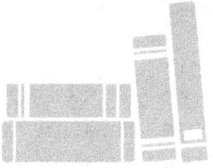

THE IDYLLS OF THE KING

LANCELOT AND ELAINE

PLOT ANALYSIS

Arthur held a yearly "diamond tournament" at which he awarded to the winning knight one of the diamonds from a crown he had found in the wilderness. Lancelot had won all but the last one, and was saving them to give to Guinevere. She was too ill to attend the last diamond tournament, however, and Lancelot felt she wished him to stay behind with her. He lied to Arthur that an old wound hindered him, but Guinevere, instead of being pleased, berated him for causing gossip by staying with her. They decided Lancelot should go anonymously to the tournament, so Arthur would attribute his change of heart to a knightly whim and not to deceit.

Wandering to the tournament by unfamiliar paths, Lancelot lost his way. He stopped at the Castle of Astolat and was welcomed by the Lord of Astolat and his two sons, Sir Torre and Sir Lavaine, as well as his daughter, the fair Elaine. During his brief visit, Lancelot regaled his hosts with stories of Arthur's court and great battles. Listening, Elaine fell in love with him, and Lavaine was fired with desire to imitate these knightly deeds. Lancelot borrowed Torre's blank shield and left his own in Elaine's keeping. Fearing people would recognize him if he wore no lady's favor (for Lancelot was known by this eccentricity) Lancelot accepted Elaine's red sleeve to tie on his helmet.

At the tournament, Lancelot, as was his practice, overthrew all who came against him. Angered at the supposed blot on the honor of their great Lancelot, his own relatives swooped down upon the nameless knight. Lancelot received from one of them a near-mortal spear wound in the side, and rode off with Lavaine before Arthur could award him the diamond. An ex-knight, turned hermit, tended Lancelot for many weeks in a cave near Camelot.

Arthur, having sent Sir Gawain after the unknown knight to award him the prize, came home to Guinevere. She informed him that the knight was Lancelot, and he told her of the lady's favor Lancelot had worn, and of his wound. In a jealous rage, Guinevere heard the news, and almost betrayed her emotion to Arthur.

Gawain, who had undertaken the quest for Lancelot unwillingly, came to Astolat. From him Elaine learned of Lancelot's wound. Gawain tried in vain to win Elaine's affection, but desisted when he realized she loved Lancelot. Leaving the diamond in her care to give Lancelot, Gawain returned to Camelot to face Arthur's anger at his disobedience.

With Sir Torre as guide, Elaine rode to Lancelot's side to nurse him. She could not help revealing her love, which disturbed the hero, but she nursed him well and saved his life by her constancy.

In his sickness, Lancelot vowed within himself to reform his life, but when well, fell back into his old sin. Though he had promised to grant Elaine any boon, he would not honor her request to become his wife. Instead he returned to Guinevere, who was so angry at his rumored betrayal that she threw his diamonds in the river right before his eyes. Elaine meanwhile had died of a broken heart, and her body was sent on a boat down the very river into which the diamonds had been thrown. A letter in the dead girl's hands to Lancelot made it clear that her love for him was unrequited. The queen therefore forgave him, but Lancelot mused bitterly on the contrast between the pure love of Elaine and the fickle love of Guinevere. Arthur confessed amazement that Lancelot had not married a girl so evidently made for him by God, unable to see why such perfection of beauty, purity and virtue had not inspired love. Lancelot struggled inwardly with his own guilt and his inability to overcome it, not dreaming that he was destined to die a holy man.

CHARACTER ANALYSES

Lancelot

Though "bruised and bronzed" and subject to violent, despairing moods, Lancelot is the soul of knightly beauty and romance. Courtesy is so ingrained in his character that it is only by a conscious effort that he can offend anyone. When Elaine's father begs him to turn Elaine's love aside, Lancelot complies by not bidding Elaine farewell, only a slight discourtesy, but one which comes hard to one of his gentle nature. Secure in his masculine strength, he finds it easy to be obedient to a woman. Yet he has lost the old belief in feminine purity because of his association with Guinevere. Even his recognition of Elaine's innocence cannot cure his cynicism. He no longer holds spiritual things higher than the profane. To avoid giving Elaine himself, he tries to put her off with an offer of material wealth. Still, he holds Arthur in unchanging love, respecting his virtue, and suffering because he is betraying so noble a friend.

Elaine

Called by her father a "willful girl," Elaine has an uncompromising character. She is utterly devoted to the ideal of purity, and offers a love so intense that it cannot be satisfied with a mere occasional friendship such as Lancelot offers in return. Her ideal is lived out in fantasy; alone with Lancelot's shield, she nurses her love of the ideal until it is shattered by reality. She refuses to believe that Lancelot loves the wife of another man, for to her, he embodies the perfection of knighthood, and she never varies from belief in all ideals. Despite the premonition that her willfulness will mean her death, Elaine persists in her love for Lancelot. Even when he does not return her love and, in his delirium, speaks roughly to her, Elaine cannot be moved. For such a resolute and determined soul, the only end possible is death itself, since the purpose of her life has been frustrated by Lancelot's rejection.

Guinevere

Perversely repelled by Arthur's superior purity and goodness, Guinevere clings to the more human, earthly passion of Lancelot. Guinevere admits that Arthur is nobler than Lancelot. She believes that the ideal of the Round Table and its "impossible vows" has divided Arthur from her, simply because she is not the center of Arthur's life as she is of Lancelot's. When she thinks she has been replaced by a rival free to marry her lover, Guinevere flies into a rage which Lancelot himself recognizes as "jealous pride." Her illicit passion and her fear of discovery have produced in Guinevere a fickle, violent disposition, contrasting with the serenity of the temperament of the "blameless Arthur." Instead of trusting Lancelot's love, Guinevere loses faith and shows her contempt for him by throwing aside his precious diamonds. The selfishness and pride of her rebellious love are apparent even to her lover.

Gawain

Contaminated by the very fact that he is Modred's brother and Lot's son, Gawain is a deceitful knight. He does not obey his king gladly or fulfill his responsibility properly. His mind is on pleasure and glory, not on virtue. Elaine attracts him, but only as the object of a flirtation, not with the holy love she deserves. Angry with Arthur for making him leave the banquets and celebrations after the tournament, Gawain treats his quest to deliver the precious diamond as a burden, not a privilege. He uses words smoothly and deceitfully, and is not a man of action like Lancelot.

Comment

The action of "Lancelot and Elaine" is built around a series of symbols: the tower, the diamonds, the shield, the river and the hermit's cave. As the inhabitant of a tower, Elaine possesses certain qualities of which the tower is symbolic. She is superior to the common run of humanity, and serves as a link between earth and heaven, to bind Lancelot to a joint fulfillment of his spiritual and earthly destinies, if he would allow her to. The diamond is a symbol of light and of mystical and moral wisdom; since it comes from Arthur's hand and is destined for Lancelot, the diamond becomes a sign of Lancelot's integrity and real purpose in life. It is given to Elaine to keep for him, for only Elaine loves him more than herself, with a love which does not dishonor him or hinder his salvation. As soon as Guinevere lays hands on the diamond, she throws it away, which indicates that Lancelot's honor and his soul are not safe in her keeping.

Like the diamond, Lancelot's shield, a sign of his identity and his power, is confided to the care of Elaine. Lancelot ultimately realizes that Guinevere is more concerned for her own reputation than for his happiness, and that Elaine's love offered him more than Guinevere's. He finds no purpose in his glory as Arthur's greatest knight because he knows his honor has been sullied by sin. Only Elaine remains true to her ideal and does not compromise her love or her honor, as do Guinevere and Lancelot. Thus, the diamonds are thrown into the river, just as her body comes to rest at Camelot, as if they were meant for her.

The river stands for loss, for the passage of time and its gifts into oblivion. When Guinevere throws Lancelot's diamonds into the river, she throws away all that was best of what he had to give her. She shows Lancelot that she no longer values him as a person and thus she puts an end to the idyllic, faithful period of romantic love they had known in the past. By committing her body to the river, Elaine reveals the irrevocable loss to Lancelot of genuine and honorable love's blessings. Lancelot can no longer hope to redeem his life in a happy, creative, and constructive manner, for time has swept the opportunity past him, like the river carries away the diamonds.

Since Lancelot has forfeited one form of redemption, his only hope lies in a future rejection of the joys of this world. Lancelot, though a success as a knight to all outward appearances, has failed to integrate earth and heaven, body and spirit, in one perfect unity. He must experience the emptiness of all life's joys before he is able to judge life purely and honestly. When he lies near physical death, he is cured at the hermit's cave, with its chapel carved from the rock by the holy man's own hands. Later, he is to be saved from spiritual death by the withdrawal from the world which a hermit's cave represents.

ESSAY QUESTION AND ANSWER

Question: In "Lancelot and Elaine," what is the fate of the Arthurian ideal which aims at uniting the spiritual with the earthly?

Answer: With "Lancelot and Elaine," the zenith of the *Idylls* has been passed, and the hope of the earlier period is clearly unrealized. The marriage of Arthur and Guinevere, which symbolically represented the mission of Arthur and the fulfillment of the heavenly ideal in earthly terms, is in the process of collapse. Guinevere is convinced that the king does not care for her, and is confident in her power over Lancelot. The diamonds which Arthur hands over to the greatest knight in his kingdom, symbolizing the union of spiritual excellence with physical prowess and valor, are thrown away by the queen. Lancelot, the foremost knight of the Round Table, is tortured by his illicit love: instead of serving his ideal, he mocks it by his betrayal of Arthur and Elaine. Guinevere betrays the ideal because in her pride and selfishness she is not content with the love of a man she knows is the noblest. Like Lancelot, she allows the earthly aspect of life to divide her from the spiritual or ideal, instead of to unite her to it, as a perfect marriage would have done.

Matters have decayed so far at Camelot that the only characters who fulfill the ideal must go to extremes: they must seek the wholly spiritual and reject all hope of its fulfillment in the world. The hermit who has withdrawn from active, knightly life is a "success," and he sets the pattern for Lancelot. Elaine leaves the world, in which her ideal was unrealizable, in death, and Arthur is to follow her example at the *Idylls*' end. They both leave the world by boat. Here, water is a symbol for physical dissolution and death, while the ideal lives on (as does Arthur's soul) as a purely spiritual being, apart from the world of the flesh.

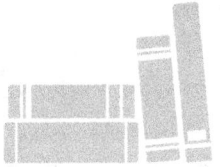

THE IDYLLS OF THE KING

GUINEVERE

PLOT ANALYSIS

Sir Modred, filled with hatred of Sir Lancelot through no fault of the noble knight, set in motion several schemes to topple Arthur from the throne. He fomented feuds within the circle of the Round Table and sought to bring the heathen down upon the realm. Fearing him, Guinevere began to feel uneasy that he would find a way to betray her illicit love to the King. At last she could no longer bear the double burden of guilt and fear, and decided that Lancelot must return to his own land. The lovers met one last time, but their tryst had been betrayed to Modred by Vivien, and Modred surrounded their tower with his knights. Even though Lancelot wounded Modred so severely that his creatures had to carry their evil master away, it was clear that Modred now had witnesses to prove Guinevere's betrayal. Lancelot begged Guinevere to flee with him to his castle, but she was determined not to compound her sin, and fled alone to the convent at Almesbury.

While Guinevere hid in the convent, Arthur finished his battle and returned home to find his wife gone. Hearing from

Modred that Guinevere had gone with Lancelot, Arthur went off to besiege the runaways, and left Modred behind in charge of the realm. Even to Guinevere, weeping in her convent, rumors came that Modred had allied himself with the heathen against the King. She had entered the convent telling no one her name, and the innocent prattle of the little novice who kept her company wounded her deeply. The novice reflected the shock and horror felt by the common people over Guinevere's betrayal of Arthur and the consequent ruin of the kingdom. Unable to bear the painful chatter of the novice any longer, Guinevere drove her away in anger. She then blamed herself for her oversensitivity and recognized that it was guilt which made her so nervous. Even though Guinevere realized that she must repent and put the past out of her mind, she could not help reminiscing about the early days of her romance with Lancelot. Just as she was recalling the cold impression that Arthur had first made upon her, the King himself came to call on his erring wife.

As Arthur spoke to her in a lifeless, ghostlike voice, Guinevere crouched before him on the floor, hiding her head in silence. First Arthur described the ruin Guinevere had brought upon the kingdom, but then his anger softened. He told her that he would leave knights to guard her while he went off to the battle which he believed would cause his doom. Arthur believed the Round Table could never be the same again because of the bad example set by those who occupied the highest places. Even though he still loved Guinevere, he could not take her back lest others be scandalized at his tolerance of evil. He forgave her and blessed her, praying that they would meet and love again in heaven.

Arthur left to fight Modred and the heathen Lords of the White Horse, and Guinevere watched him from a window. Now that it was too late, she knew she loved her husband. He was more human than she had believed, and he loved her more than she had known. When the novice came to her weeping, begging to be forgiven now that she knew Guinevere's true identity, the queen forgave her as she herself had been forgiven. Afterwards, she lived a holy life, dying as abbess of the convent.

CHARACTER ANALYSES

Guinevere

Despite the accusations of the novice, Guinevere insists to herself that her love is not evil and that Lancelot is an ideal knight. She is so dependent on her illusions, that she cannot give them up even after she has resolved to repent. Her passions are not hers to control; they oblige her mind to dwell lovingly on the happy days of her romance with Lancelot. Because Arthur does not make as much fuss over her as Lancelot did, Guinevere loves him less, for she is both proud and vain. After she realizes the extent of Arthur's virtue and goodness, she sees in a flash that she has allowed the lower side of her nature to distract her from the highest good. Always quick to be moved by her passions, Guinevere acts whole-heartedly on her new insight and inspiration, and ends her life in holiness, though she had spent it in the opposite state.

Arthur

The King is a man dominated by his conscience, which in turn is the conscience of his country and his knights. Because he has perfect control over his passions, he appears cold to those who do not know his heart. Though he loves Guinevere, he loves God and Duty more. Thus, he cannot take her back, however much he wishes to. His mission is totally bound up with his love for his wife; and when she proves unfaithful, he knows his doom is near. For Arthur, a man's service to humanity is inspired by his love for his lady and his desire to spread her fame. Though wounded to the death by her infidelity, Arthur speaks only a few brief condemnatory lines. Quickly his wrath and sorrow are subdued, and he thinks only of the soul of the person lying before him. He remembers his one-time happiness with her and longs for heaven, when they can put aside their baser natures and love purely and perfectly. He knows his own worth, and declares that Guinevere will someday realize that Lancelot is a lesser man than himself. Arthur rises above the natural desire for revenge. His heart is single-minded; where it has once loved, it loves forever. Therefore, he is not ashamed to tell Guinevere that she cannot change his love by her deeds. Even in heaven, Arthur declares, he will love her still.

Comment

The cycle of Arthur's era is rapidly drawing to a close. The "creeping mist" clings to the "dead earth," as destruction, death and dissolution prevail over the order wrought by Arthur's earlier years. Modred's rebellion is open, not hidden as it was when Arthur's star was high. The final sign of the approaching end is Arthur's farewell to his wife. When he has left the convent where she lives, his face is "as an angel's." Having severed his last bond with the flesh in which his very life and mission were incarnate, Arthur becomes pure spirit, ready for his doom. Guinevere sees the mist encompass him "till himself became as mist," and his form seems "the phantom of a Giant." Mist or water signals doom for Arthur, because it is from water that he has come and to water that he must return. Here water is a sign of mystical rebirth, a baptism into his new way of life on a new level of existence.

Both Guinevere and Arthur are keenly aware that it was only through their perfect love and marriage that redemption could be accomplished in the realm. Love was to bring forth fruit: a holy, happy kingdom, mirroring the joy of the marriage itself. Arthur does not sorrow over his lost love only for personal reasons; he knows that his entire mission depended on his marriage. He says to the penitent Guinevere: "Thou hast spoilt the purpose of my life." When she has lost him, Guinevere is equally able to perceive the magnitude of her sin: "Ah my God, / What might I not have made of thy fair world. / Had I but loved thy highest creature here?" If we assume Arthur represents the soul or conscience, and Guinevere represents the body, it is clear that the idyll has an allegorical dimension. When the flesh goes its own way, as it does in the case of Tristram, and denies its spiritual obligations, ruin follows for both the individual and society. Guinevere and Arthur were intended to form one person by their union, and to set an example of perfect harmony and integrity. Instead, the watching world finds the union a failure and goes on to divorce itself from ideals completely. When Arthur parts from Guinevere, his realm loses its soul, and the natural order of the world loses its sustaining spirit of idealism. All that remains is for the realm to dissolve in anarchy and bloodshed.

ESSAY QUESTIONS AND ANSWERS

Question: What images are used to indicate decay and disaster in "Guinevere"?

Answer: The end of an era is unmistakably marked by natural phenomena. The mists of autumn hang over the land and all vegetation is dead. The cold wind sweeps over a desolate landscape, and Guinevere hears a raven croak as she flees to Almesbury by night. The raven and the wind represent to her the spoiling of the land by the heathen. As if by wind, the beauty and order spread by Arthur over his realm are swept away, while the mindless croaking of a black bird remains to comment on the death of light and spirit. The little novice sings to Guinevere a song which recalls the "Parable of the Wise and the Foolish Virgins": "O let us in, that we may find the light! / Too later, too late: ye cannot enter now." Guinevere, with all the lost sheep of Arthur's flock, stands in the darkness outside the heaven of Arthur's powerful presence. Guinevere dreams that she is standing before a setting sun, which is symbolic of Arthur in his decline. Something vile brushes her, and then she is aware that her own shadow has spread and is consuming the land as if by fire. The symbols of sun, darkness and fire convey in rapid strokes the picture of Guinevere's betrayal and the ruin which is its result.

Question: What is the pattern of Guinevere's conversion and redemption?

Answer: Guinevere begins her detachment from the world of the senses with vague surges of fear and guilt. No longer does her romance bring her pleasure. More and more she is afraid of betrayal and guilt-ridden over the blow she has dealt her King and her kingdom. As her fears grow more intense, she is at last able to part with the person who is the object of her sinful desires. She comes to this gesture of renunciation not out of high motives of love for virtue or unselfishness, but out of fear for her reputation and her queenly status. Once all is lost and Modred has caught them in the tower, Guinevere rises to a new level of moral insight. Instead of fleeing with Lancelot as he invites her to do, she recognizes that he cannot hide her from her own guilt. She now sees herself and her sin clearly enough to desire to sin no more.

Now Guinevere knows that had Arthur found a woman as great as himself, the two of them might have remade the world. A growing awareness of divine regret, larger than mere self-pity, takes possession of her soul, and she is filled with sorrow for her role in the realm's ruin, as well as for her failure to perfect her own life by loving the highest, purest person in it. No longer does she excuse her love for Lancelot; she admits that Arthur had every right to claim her total fidelity. By this admission, Guinevere puts aside the illusory veil of romance and sees reality clearly. The experience is for her a true rebirth. In entering Almesbury anonymously, Guinevere separates herself physically from Arthur and her married life, and she loses her old identity. When she assumes her name once again, it is as a new personality, one redeemed by confession of sin and perfect sorrow for it.

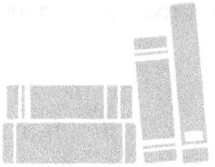

THE IDYLLS OF THE KING

THE COMING OF ARTHUR

| PLOT ANALYSIS

Britain was a land of petty princes, warring against one another since imperial Rome had retreated from the island. King Leodogran of Cameliard's kingdom had been laid waste, both by the heathen Norsemen from across the sea and by the battling kings of Britain. In despair, he asked the aid of young Arthur, newly made king, though Arthur had never taken arms before or proved himself in battle. Even while Arthur was away from home to help Leodogran, rebellious knights plotted against him, doubting his right to rule. As Arthur fought the older king's battle, his mind dwelled on Guinevere, the king's only child and the fairest lady in the land. Already, though he had seen her only once, he knew she must be his wife.

Arthur won his battles against all Leodogran's enemies. With this victory he also won Lancelot's recognition of his divine right to rule, and the two swore fidelity till death. At once the king sent three knights to ask Leodogran for Guinevere's hand, but Leodogran was reluctant to agree until he learned more of Arthur's parentage. Two of his old servants told him that only from Bleys, an ancient sage, or his pupil Merlin, could such a truth be learned. Leodogran questioned the three knights sent by Arthur to learn what they thought of his royal qualifications. Bedivere, foremost among Arthur's knights, declared that only those evil men who desired to destroy Arthur out of envy for his goodness questioned Arthur's right to be their lord. He recommended that Leodogran learn more from Bellicent, Arthur's sister.

From Bedivere, Leodogran learned the story of Arthur that was public knowledge. King Uther had fallen in love with Ygerne, wife of Gorlais, and fought her husband to the death in order to marry her. Soon afterward he died, bewailing his lack of an heir. On the same night, which also began the new year, Arthur was born. Because of the infant's danger from power-hungry knights, Merlin spirited him away, to be raised as the foster child of sir Anton. When later Merlin brought Arthur forth to be crowned, grumblers claimed Arthur was only the son of Gorlais or Anton. His coronation caused open warfare.

Leodogran, still unconvinced, consulted with Bellicent, recently arrived at Cameliard with her two young sons, Gawain and Modred. Bellicent assured Leodogran that Arthur was a true king, and that divine power dwelled with him, guaranteed by the presence at court of the Lady of the Lake (giver of Arthur's sword, Excalibur), Merlin the wizard, and three fairy queens. Questioned further, Bellicent told first her happy memories of Arthur's kindness to her during their childhood, and finally the story she had heard about his origins from Bleys before his death. Bleys had told her of how Merlin, upon Uther's death, had gone out to the seashore with Bleys, and there had seen momentarily a dragon-shaped ship, bearing "shining people." A fiery wave bore a naked baby to Merlin, who seized the child and named him king. This child was Arthur. Leodogran, considering these things, dreamed that night of a king upon a mountain peak, repudiated by voices from below, yet finally triumphant in heaven. This decided Leodogran, and he agreed to give Guinevere to Arthur.

Arthur had Lancelot bring Guinevere from Cameliard, and they were married in the spring by Saint Dubric. Immediately, the Roman envoys entered Arthur's hall, demanding tribute, but he sent them away. The old had given place to the new, and now Arthur, not Rome, defended a united Britain.

CHARACTER ANALYSES

King Arthur

The personification of masculine strength and religious devotion, Arthur embodies a Christ-like ideal that impresses itself on the men around him. Though brave in a just war, Arthur is reluctant to resort to killing, a fact which is revealed by his sadness at receiving Excalibur. His whole impulse is to create harmony, order and justice in his realm. He is identified with both Christ and the sun, the sources of spiritual and earthly life.

Guinevere

As the embodiment of the physical world in its beauty and vitality, Guinevere is both woman and earth. She regards only outward traits of people. When Arthur rides past her, dressed as simply as his men, she does not recognize him because he is not garbed in the trappings of royalty. Her values are those of the world, not of the spirit.

Lancelot

While he served the king in war, Lancelot could not truly accept Arthur's royal claim until Arthur had proved himself in battle. Like Guinevere, Lancelot relies upon experience, not intuition or faith, to carry him through life. Arthur loves him better than any other man, and loves him for himself; but Lancelot only loves Arthur for the sake of Arthur's glorious deeds.

Bellicent

Queen Bellicent is tender-minded, feminine and full of intuitive faith in Arthur and his mission. She believes in him out of family loyalty, personal experience, and the witness of the seer Bleys to Arthur's supernatural origin. Her loyalty is emotional rather than a matter of steady willpower, and in the end we shall see that emotion leads her to doubt Arthur's claim.

Merlin

In the first idyll, Merlin is seen only through the eyes of others. Bellicent sees him as a maddening maker of riddles and recounts his exploit with the infant Arthur, when both were bathed in supernatural flames. Thus Bellicent's Merlin emerges as a superhuman seer. Bedivere sees Merlin as a shrewd and thoughtful servant of the kingdom, who ensures an heir to the throne.

Leodogran

Guinevere's father is seen only as an old man unable to fight his enemies, yet concerned to do his duty and protect his realm.

He is also concerned for the happiness of his daughter, and is unwilling to give her to a man whose noble birth is a matter for doubt. Because he doubts, Leodogran intelligently seeks evidence so that he may make a proper judgment. His reluctance serves as an opportune device for the revealing of Arthur's background to the reader.

Comment

From the beginning of the poem, when Leodogran first decides to send for Arthur, the question of Arthur's origin is raised. This is the central mystery of the first idyll, into which we are plunged deeper and deeper until Bellicent's revelation makes it clear that Arthur's origin is supernatural. The question of Arthur's authority is implicit in the nature of his origin; those who deny Arthur's authority claim to do so on the basis of his doubtful parentage. Actually, such men deny Arthur because he represents virtue, and they want nothing to do with virtue. Since Tennyson desired, in the *Idylls*, to defend the Christian faith and its ideals against the onslaught of rationalism, it is probable that Arthur can be regarded as a Christ figure, among other things.

If Tennyson meant to equate the rejection of Arthur and his supernatural claim with the rejection of Christ and His, he is also saying that doubt is only superficially reasonable and actually due to malice and egotism. Those who accept Arthur do so for several reasons. Bellicent believes in him because she has faith in the miraculous story told by Bleys and because she has experienced the warmth of Arthur's love. Her belief is a type of Christian faith mixed with an intuitive experience of divine love. Lancelot, and Gareth in the next idyll, believe in Arthur out of respect for his deeds, a type of faith based on objective scrutiny of the hero's pattern of life and action in order to determine the presence of divinity.

The sword, Excalibur, had the words "To act or not to act" emblazoned upon it. They represent Arthur's first dilemma. Throughout his life he will be confronted by this problem, in which his gentle nature is in conflict with the necessity for violence in the keeping of the peace. When we initially see Arthur, it is against the background of chaos, despair and hate. The Britain he is to rule is a land laid waste. Arthur's first venture into action, his first involvement in the muddied waters of the world's suffering, takes place at the poem's beginning, and it involves Guinevere. Throughout the *Idylls*, Arthur must function in the world united to Guinevere, who stands for the earth, the flesh, the feminine principle, and for the real, visible world in which the ideal or the idea must operate. Arthur, as an ideal figure representing the masculine principle, must be joined to Guinevere if he is to act and create order out of chaos. Having won Guinevere and having united Britain, Arthur completes this achievement of order by killing wild beasts, leveling forests and making paths through them. He fulfills the human and divine idea of integrity and order, symbolized by the Round Table. The circle has always been a symbol of divine perfection and indivisible unity, and Arthur's table thus takes on cosmic dimensions because of its shape.

As Arthur is symbolic of Christ, of the soul and of devout humanity in general, so Excalibur is symbolic of Arthur. It rises from the water in a fairy's hand, just as Arthur is borne to Merlin on the waves of the sea, presumably having come from the fairy ship. Ultimately the sword will be reclaimed by the fairy hand in the water, to signal the end of Arthur's cycle, just as Arthur himself leaves the known, physical world by water. In his riddles, Merlin refers to Arthur's cyclic pattern: Arthur is to return to the "deep" from which he has come, and he is to come again. In the dream of Leodogran, Arthur is triumphant in heaven even while on earth men deny his claims. The cycle of Arthur must end with death and a transfiguration in the next life, just as did the history of Christ. The cycle is emphasized and deepened in significance by the fact that Arthur comes in the beginning of the new year, and dies on the same occasion at the cycle's close. Temporal events also serve to point out the cyclic nature of the *Idylls*: Arthur drives the Romans away, declaring that the old must give place to the new, and that as Rome had had its day, so must Britain have hers. Here, and throughout the *Idylls*, Arthur is established as the spirit of Britain and its most representative hero.

ESSAY QUESTIONS AND ANSWERS

Question: How is Arthur's character marked by trust or faith, and how does this quality affect his dealings with others?

Answer: Arthur is able to trust others completely because he himself is without guile. Innocence of deceit is one of the chief marks of beauty of character in the *Idylls*: we will see it again in Elaine and in Galahad. Such innocence is always holy, but it does not always gain worldly success for its possessor. Arthur freely gives his whole trust to Lancelot, saying: "Man's word is God in man. / Let chance what will, I trust thee to the death." Arthur perceives that man's closest likeness to divinity is his capacity for faith. In order to act at all, Arthur, like any man, must perform an act of faith. He must believe that action is worth the trouble it takes to engage in it. Once Arthur decides to act, he trusts in action implicitly, and does not waver in his fidelity to the world or its symbol, Guinevere. Because of his faith in others, Arthur often acts through them. He sends

Bedivere to ask for Guinevere and he sends Lancelot to bring her to court. Like Christ, Arthur must depend on men for the realization of his mission, and he willingly extends his faith to them as he does his love.

Question: What are the religious symbols Tennyson uses to invest Arthur and his kingship with supernatural overtones?

Answer: The religious guarantees of Arthur's claims on men's loyalty are primarily expressed through the persons of fairies surrounding him. Chief among these is the Lady of the Lake, who is given the character and role of the Holy Spirit. She comes from the water, the source of all life and its end; thus she can be said to come symbolically from God Himself. Three queens, touched with a heavenly light, stand near Arthur's throne, friends ready to help him. This light and the fire in which the infant Arthur appears, as well as the "shining people" from whose boat Arthur came, are related to divine being and divine enlightenment. The tongues of fire present over the heads of the Apostles at the coming of the Holy Spirit are similar religious symbols of divine mission and inspiration.

Two of the chief symbols bound to Arthur's person are the Round Table and the sword. The roundness of the table can be viewed as a symbol for the perfection and serenity of God the Father, resting in Himself in beatific contemplation. The sword, with its hilt like a cross, represents divine action in the world, which complements interior rest and peace (symbolized by the Table). At a table, one rests and is nourished; with the sword, or on the Cross, one engages in the violence and sufferings of everyday life. As the Table is symbolic of the Father, so the sword is the Son. Arthur needs them both to perform his role, just as he needs the Lady of the Lake's presence to maintain his divine inspiration.

THE IDYLLS OF THE KING

THE HOLY GRAIL

PLOT ANALYSIS

Having left Arthur's court and entered a monastery, Sir Percivale told the curious Brother Ambrosius the following story.

Percivale's sister, unlucky in love, had become a nun. She determined to fast and pray until she saw the Holy Grail. When she succeeded, she convinced her brother, who in turn convinced many of the knights of the Round Table, to leave the things of this world, and devote their lives to a purely spiritual quest. Galahad enjoyed a holy friendship with Percivale's sister, who regarded him as her spiritual brother, and even wove for him a swordbelt out of hair shorn from her own head. Galahad then dared to sit in the "Siege perilous" at the Round Table, which brought about a violent thunder storm, and then, in a bright beam of light, the Holy Grail appeared to him. The other knights determined to become pure enough to see the vision, and vowed to follow Galahad's example. Arthur then returned from a quest to avenge an "outraged maiden" who had been attacked by bandits. He was distressed to learn of the vow, for he realized that it meant the ruin of the Round Table and the death of many good knights.

To mark the occasion, Arthur decreed a Tournament, won by Galahad and Percivale.

The next day, the departing knights were seen off by a court which wept over its loss. Guinevere in particular cried aloud that it was their sins that had caused the **catastrophe**. Percivale, finding himself quickly in a desolate country of "sand and thorns," groaned that the quest was not destined for him. When he rode on and came to meadows with orchards, a simple peasant woman, a knight in golden armor, and finally a glorious city where voices welcomed him as a pure and mighty man - all these earthly goods turned to dust before him. He feared that the Grail itself might do the same, should he ever find it. At last he found a hermit near a chapel, who told him that he was not utterly pure and selfless like Galahad. Galahad, youngest of the knights, had spent his quest in doing good works wherever he went. At this point, Galahad himself appeared, entered the chapel to pray, and saw again the vision of the Grail. Percivale, who still had seen nothing, went on with Galahad, as his attendant and spiritual heir. Together, they climbed a steep mountain; and then Percivale watched Galahad cross an evil-smelling swamp by an ancient path, spring through fire, and finally enter the heavenly city in the light of that Grail which all pursued but which none would ever see again. Percivale, having seen the Grail over his friend's head, abandoned the world for a hermitage.

Pressed by Ambrosius to reveal whether or not he had met flesh-and-blood persons on his quest, Percivale admitted that he had seen one woman. He had loved her in his youth and then, on the quest, met her as a rich widow, needing his love and protection. Because of the quest, he left her. He also ran across the good knight Sir Bors, who reported that Lancelot rode like a grim madman in pursuit of the Grail, without hope of success. Sir Bors himself had been captured by a primitive tribe, and while suffering in his prison, had seen the Grail. When Percivale returned to the court, he found all had fallen out as Arthur foretold: a gale had destroyed the great hall and those few knights who had returned from their quests were weakened by their austerities. Gawain, who had made the vow in a louder voice than the others, had given up the quest. Instead, he had dallied in a silk tent with some maidens, until the gale blew it apart. Lancelot had found the tower where the Grail was kept, but was kept by fire from seeing any more than a veiled shape. Arthur blessed them for their efforts, but deplored the loss to the realm which had come because men would not combine mystical holiness with duties toward mankind.

CHARACTER ANALYSES

Ambrosius

Though he had embraced the spiritual life, Ambrosius has no illusions about it. He sees that men who do not help to create and preserve the world are incompletely developed in personality and character.

Percivale

Second only to Galahad among Arthur's knights in purity, Percivale is recognized for his virtue and prowess by all who knew him. He is a man fiercely driven by a single passion, which rules out all others. Despite his love for the young widow, her need of him and Arthur's warning that the quest might be in vain, he leaves her behind. For this deed, he "hated himself," and he weeps at the realization of the joy he has lost. Percival consistently refuses to gratify the strongest and most legitimate of his earthly desires, in order to follow the examples of his holy sister and of Galahad. It is not enough that he imitate the king and devote himself to good works; he cannot rest content with such a "compromise" and determines to cut all that is not spiritual out of his life.

Sir Bors

An unselfish, humble knight, Sir Bors would have preferred that his beloved relative, Lancelot, receive the vision instead of himself. His honest, forthright, practical soul was intended by God for a joyful, useful life in the world, but the quest had made this impossible. Instead, Sir Bors is sad despite his courteous smile. His brave defense of his holy pilgrimage against the pagan priests results in his suffering. In turn, this "martyrdom" gives him the right to the vision he seeks.

Galahad

Rumored to be the son of Lancelot, Galahad is perfect in every way, possessing that supernatural purity that Lancelot had forfeited by his guilty love for the queen. He believes absolutely in the merit of the quest, for he accepts on faith the word of the holy nun he loves as a sister. In his complete faith, he does not hesitate to sit in the Siege Perilous and to dissent from King Arthur about the ultimate aim of human life. Galahad's ideals are celibacy and mysticism. Arthur keeps prayer and good works in equal balance with one another, while Galahad desires to leave the world behind him so that prayer can be practiced to the exclusion of everything else. Unlike the other knights, however, Galahad enjoys the constant presence of the Grail and, as he travels, fights battles in defense of the good. Ultimately, however, he pursues the Grail beyond life, beyond this world, and voluntarily abandons his vocation in the world of Arthur's court.

Sir Lancelot

Pursuing the Grail with the same unrestrained madness as he pursues the glory of knighthood and the love of Guinevere, Lancelot is unable to rid himself of the earthly quality which the queen so loves in him. In his self-deception, he hopes to gain freedom from his sin by touching the Grail, not by an act of will. As he travels in search of that heavenly sign, the Grail, Lancelot is overwhelmed by lesser knights, and the sword is ultimately struck from his hand. Violence gives way to humility and self-knowledge. He perceives the nature of his sin and desires to cleanse himself of it, for he sees that all his honor is compromised and corrupted by this one evil.

Sir Gawain

"Reckless and irreverent," Gawain is quick to give up the quest for the sake of the pleasures of the flesh. Unlike Arthur, he objects to the quest because of sensuality, not duty. Arthur knows Gawain is a boaster, and that those who seek the Grail are far worthier than the knight who mocks them.

Comment

In "The Holy Grail," the division between the real and the ideal becomes sharper than ever before. Arthur's mission is to teach a perfect fusion of the active life and the contemplative life to the little world which is his court. His knights are supposed to look to him for example, but they look instead to Galahad, showing their lack of faith in Arthur's ideals. Arthur attempted to pursue the goal in a married state, and wished others to do likewise. Since Arthur's marriage is now an obvious failure, Galahad's celibate, mystical ideal seems the only possible model upon which an honorable knight can build his life. Yet Galahad is a special case, as Arthur himself admitted. The contemplative life is for the few, and not for everyone; it is the Siege Perilous, which only Galahad can safely occupy. For lesser men, it is a way of death, not life. Galahad succeeds in his quest because of his own purity and because he has contracted a new kind of "marriage," where the masculine and feminine unite only in the mystical union of prayer. He and Percivale's sister are able to find the Grail, symbol of Christian sanctity and heavenly perfection, because they are linked together. Galahad is even bound about the waist by a ring of her hair, symbolizing his borrowing from her spiritual strength and resources in order to carry out his quest.

While his knights babble in excitement over Galahad's vision, and make their foolish vow, Arthur is doing his duty. The girl he is avenging is "smear'd with earth," her clothes are torn. She is the bitter reality which all but Arthur try to avoid, for they prefer to seek the ideal divorced from common life. Ambrosius, the monk, speaks with the voice of wisdom, echoing Arthur and affirming that a celibate life is cold and lonely, removed from life as it is really lived. Ambrosius himself leaves the monastery to associate with common people, and so maintains the proper balance between contemplation and charity to one's fellow man. Arthur and the wise monk do not seek an ideal divorced from reality, but one incarnate within it. Arthur describes his own mystical life as union of duty with love of God, in which the soul is unconscious of itself and its beatitude, and lives in the perpetual light and joy of God the Father. He is a complete human being with perfect integrity because his personality has never been dominated by either the heavenly vision or the duty imposed by his earthly vocation. Both aspects of his life are developed and they complement one another. Arthur believes visions should not be sought for their own sake, but received as a blessing when God chooses to send them to a man who does his duty.

ESSAY QUESTIONS AND ANSWERS

Question: How does the dual nature of the search for the Holy Grail reflect the clashing sets of values in the *Idylls*?

Answer: The quest is not only performed as an outward pilgrimage, but also represents a journey into the depths of the souls of individual men. Sir Percivale reveals this dual nature of the search for the Grail when he tells Ambrosius that he met no persons, only "phantoms," on his travels. For him, the search involves a personal confrontation with his own "baser" desires: for nature's beauty, the love of a good woman, knightly honor, and social and civic responsibility all become dust when he compares them to the ideal of prayerful retirement away from the world. Percivale admits that real men and women cease to exist for the true hermit, and this failure of charity reveals the difference of Galahad's ideal from that of Arthur. Yet the tragedy remains: in the adulterous, corrupted atmosphere of the court, there is no longer any possibility for the fulfillment of Arthur's ideal. Only withdrawal from the physical world can save the souls of individual men.

Question: How does "The Holy Grail" maintain and develop the cyclic motif introduced in the earlier idylls?

Answer: Percivale tells Ambrosius the story of the quest as they sit under a "world-old yew-tree" (reminiscent of the one under which Arthur Hallam was buried), which Ambrosius suggests represents the serene, unmoving central eye of the cosmos, through which the contemplative monk views the action of men in any particular time. Such a view allows a breadth of vision beyond the merely historical, one which sees the rise, decay and fall of whole cultures. Under this tree, the two monks discuss and judge the action of Arthur's knights during the period of the great quest, then relate that action to the wider context of humanity's relationship with God.

The earlier years of Christianity in Britain were blessed with the healing presence of the Grail, but sin caused the Holy Cup's disappearance. It only returned to the world as a sign that Arthur's mission to restore men's hearts to virtue had succeeded, however briefly. With the decline of the Round Table, the failure of Arthur's ideal and the ascent of Galahad to the heavenly Jerusalem, the Cup is again lost to men's eyes. Presumably, only another great cycle, in which humanity would again be blessed with a hero like Arthur, could reveal the Grail clearly to men.

Images describing the passage of immense periods of time and change appear throughout the poem. Camelot, built in past ages, has begun to crumble, and Merlin's statue of Arthur has lost one of its golden wings. Now Arthur and other men must fly to heaven on the single wing of mystical prayer, lacking the wing of creative action in the world. Galahad and Percivale travel through an ancient forest and then through a swamp which contains the bones of men. They probe into the area beyond the wasteland of the barbarians around Camelot, into the depths of the human past. On another level, they pass from the world of common passion to that of grossest instinct, plunging further and further into the depths of the human soul.

Galahad is able to perceive, even in these depths, the network of bridges built by a king in ancient times, and to follow them safely to the "great Sea." Here we seem to be moving into the abysses of human personality, into that formless place where the identity of man is mysteriously merged with the being of God. For when Galahad is upon this sea, he is caught up to the heavenly city, or "translated" from earth to heaven. In his wild flight, Galahad recapitulates the entire history of man, as well as man's individual drama of salvation. In his path from Camelot's order to the wasteland, and from there to the swamp, he traces the cycle of material decline and decay to which the Round Table is doomed. At the same time, Galahad's quest, and its ultimate success, mirrors the redemption of those individuals who leave the world (the court) and seek in death or penance the purely spiritual condition of heaven.

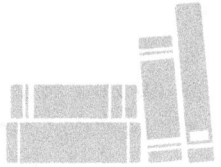

THE IDYLLS OF THE KING

PELLEAS AND ETTARRE

PLOT ANALYSIS

On his way to Camelot, Pelleas lay down to rest in a forest. As he lay there, he dreamed of the pure lady whom he would love with a perfect and holy love when he found her. Ettarre and her attendants rode by him, lost in the forest, and Pelleas, struck by her beauty, offered to be her guide. At first, he could not speak for love, and she laughed at him; but when she learned he was to compete at the tournament, she was more kind. Ettarre wanted the golden circlet to be offered to her by the winner, and promised Pelleas her love if he would win for her.

Despite his youth, Arthur made Pelleas a knight, and even withheld the older knights from the tournament so that the young man might win the trophy for his lady. Once Pelleas had won the circlet for her, Ettarre had no further use for him. She went home to her own castle, and would not admit Pelleas, who followed her faithfully. He thought he was merely being tested, for he could not imagine that a lady would break her promise. She had her knight's try first to drive him away, and then to kill him, but Pelleas overthrew them. Having found out that Ettarre wanted him brought bound into the castle, Pelleas obediently let himself be captured. Ettarre railed at him so that Pelleas feared to cause her further trouble. He would rather give her up than force her to utter such unbecoming words. As he left her, Ettarre briefly regretted her inability to love so noble a man.

Gawain chanced by and took pity on Pelleas in his plight. He offered to borrow Pelleas' armor and horse and to pretend to Ettarre that he had killed Pelleas. He planned to stay three days with Ettarre and tell her such glowing stories of Pelleas' valor that she would long for her faithful suitor to return to life.

At the end of three days, weary with waiting for Gawain, Pelleas stole into the castle courtyard and saw three tents, one of which sheltered Ettarre and Gawain, sleeping side by side. At first he wanted to kill them both, but honor forbade killing a sleeping knight, and instead he left his naked sword across the throats of the sleeping pair. In a rage he rode away from the castle, his love replaced by hatred. Ettarre awoke, and finding the sword, reproached Gawain with his lie about killing Pelleas. Perversely, she began to love the very one she had scorned, and pined in vain for him the rest of her life.

When Pelleas had left Ettarre, he encountered Percivale, from whom he learned that even Guinevere and Lancelot were false. This drove him to madness, and he fled on. In his furious flight, Pelleas rode down an old beggar, and then challenged Sir Lancelot to battle. Pelleas would not tell his name and only railed against the sin of Guinevere. Lancelot easily overcame the swordless boy, and brought Pelleas back to Camelot. When brought before Queen Guinevere, Pelleas could not even greet her. Brushing aside her inquiries, he rushed out into the night, away from the court which had so disappointed him. Lancelot and Guinevere began to recognize the harm their love had done to Arthur's court, and the evil Modred, looking on, judged that the time for rebellion was ripe.

CHARACTER ANALYSES

Pelleas

A single-minded idealist, Pelleas is ignorant of the moral decay that has taken place in Arthur's court. He himself has newly come from his island, and is like an island of innocence in Arthur's court. He is in love with love and unable to see the woman who has captured his eye for what she is. Made captive by his own idealism, he is unable to survive in a world where cynicism and betrayal dominate. Once his romantic, unrealistic ideals are destroyed, there is nothing but hatred left within him. Idealism is all that supports his virtue; and his idealism is not based on an interior faith, but on other people whom he wishes to imitate. When these others fail him, he cannot rise to Arthur's stature, but instead follows the course of bitterness and denial of all values. Ultimately, he judges even his own love as no more than "lust."

Ettarre

Vain and shrewish, Ettarre has based her life on cynicism and selfishness. Her perversity obliges her to hate when she is loved, and love when she is hated. She is attracted to spurious values, caring more for the flattery of a crude suitor than for the pure love of Pelleas. She is too cynical to believe that Pelleas would love her if he knew her as she really is, and does not care to reform her life so that she will be worthy of a good man's love.

Gawain

A healthy regard for his own interests prevents Gawain from falling victim to the ideals which inspire other knights. As a warrior, he responds to Pelleas' plight when the latter is attacked by Ettarre's knights, but when confronted with Ettarre herself, he forsakes his promise to win her for Pelleas. His character is marked by violence: he is eager to fight Ettarre's men and declares he would mutilate anyone who tried to harm him, even at his lady's request. Though he had pledged good faith to Pelleas by the Round Table itself, he is quick to betray his friend and his vows to Arthur. As a cynic, Gawain fares well in a rotting world, while Pelleas is doomed.

Comment

The tragedy of Pelleas reflects the crisis that betrayal and illicit love have brought upon Arthur's court. Pelleas himself is a lesser Arthur, who begins in innocence, loves an unworthy woman, and is destroyed by the failure of his love. Like Arthur, he comes young and innocent into the world of the court, but unlike Arthur, he has no supernatural guarantees of virtue. He meets his lady in the forest, which is, throughout the *Idylls*, a place of anarchy, trouble and sin, just as Arthur met Guinevere when her land was laid waste by battle. Arthur saves Guinevere, and Pelleas guides the lost Ettarre to the haven of Camelot, so that both heroes demonstrate their good faith by their deeds. Both of them depend on a woman's fidelity for the fulfillment of their purpose in life, and both of them are disappointed and brought to their downfall by feminine failure to love honorably.

In denying Pelleas, Ettarre repudiates Arthur also, and declares she hates the very sound of Arthur's voice. When purity and honor are rejected, so is the ideal of the Round Table and belief in the king himself. In his madness and disappointment in Ettarre, Pelleas dares to question even Arthur's purity, after which he rides down the crippled beggar as callously as Ettarre had rejected him. Virtue in the *Idylls* is dependent upon faith in the King, and unconditional acceptance of the Round Table's code of honor, regardless of the conduct of others. Pelleas justifies his own fall by noting the folly of Ettarre, Lancelot and Guinevere. His idealism is deficient and doomed, because he is not clear-sighted enough to see his own responsibility for his own virtue.

In "Pelleas and Ettarre," the idealist has become the fool. While Galahad wins heaven with an incorruptible ideal, Pelleas lives in a private hell because he is devoted to a romantic ideal. The reward of the idealist is disappointment because the Round Table is sinking into a period of decline. The moral atmosphere of the court has been so corrupted by Lancelot's and Guinevere's bad example, that cynicism is a more workable attitude at court than is idealism. When Guinevere asks Pelleas why he resents being overthrown by Lancelot, Pelleas can only hiss at her, "I have no sword." All his knightly courtesy has been stripped from him, and he has been disarmed by the betrayals all around him. He left his sword and his youthful, innocent idealism with the sleeping Ettarre and Gawain. Now, for Guinevere and all of Camelot he has only contempt.

ESSAY QUESTION AND ANSWER

Question: How do the ironic elements of "Pelleas and Ettarre" reinforce the increasing gap between the ideal and the reality at Arthur's court?

Answer: From the beginning, Pelleas' love is cursed with ironic ambiguity. His ideal is profane and not sacred; knightly glory is for him more closely involved with love than with honor. He is in love with love, not with a real woman. It is clear from the opening scene that Pelleas plans to find a woman "pure as Guinevere," to whom he will be a very Arthur, and he loves her even before he finds her. Ettarre is often referred to as a "great lady," a condition of outward honor which contrasts with her inner degradation. Like Guinevere, she seems to the naive Pelleas both great and good, while in fact both women are the opposite. **Irony** depends on the truth not being what it seems, but masked or distorted by half-truths.

When Pelleas learns the truth, his extreme idealism becomes extreme cynicism; he envies the brute animals for their insensitivity and he equates his own love with lust. The **irony** of his situation is due to the complete division at court between ideal human behavior and the real world. Pelleas responds to this division first with innocent blindness to the facts and then with cynical blindness to the values still upheld by Arthur. The promise of Gawain to win Ettarre's love for Pelleas is ironically fulfilled, despite its apparent betrayal. When Pelleas denies love and its values, Ettarre perversely learns love's value. Through the **irony** implicit in Pelleas's failure to relate his ideals to reality, the ultimate failure of the mission of Arthur becomes dramatically apparent.

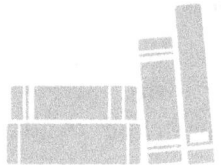

THE IDYLLS OF THE KING

THE PASSING OF ARTHUR

PLOT ANALYSIS

Lying in his tent before the great battle with Modred and the heathen, Arthur passed through a spiritual crisis in which he wondered if God were present at all in the world of men. He knew that God ruled nature, but could not find Him in humanity. Despite his anguish, Arthur was able to resolve the problem: he was only an instrument of God's will and too insignificant to be able to see the end result of the divine plan. He dreamed that he heard the ghost of Gawain, who had been killed in the war against Lancelot. This spirit wailed, as it passed through the night, that all pleasure is hollow. Arthur told Sir Bedivere, his faithful companion, that doom was certainly upon them, since only a remnant of the realm remained on the side of the King, and the King could not fight against the will of his own people.

The battle was fought in a swirling mist, and those who killed each other could not see those they killed. In the silence after the fighting, Arthur surveyed the bodies and spied Modred, maker of the carnage. The two men closed in mortal combat. Modred's lethal blow to the King was followed by Excalibur's last stroke.

Modred lay dead, and Bedivere carried the fallen King to a half-destroyed chapel on a nearby peninsula.

Arthur declared to Bedivere that the Round Table had at last been destroyed, and that he and his best knights had fallen victim to the people they had tried to save. Since he felt he could not live until morning, he ordered the knight to take Excalibur, throw the sword into the middle of the lake, and then bring back word of what happened. Bedivere promised to comply, and went to do the King's bidding. Because the sword's jewelled hilt was so beautiful, however, Bedivere hid the weapon by the water and pretended to the King that he had followed orders. Arthur knew he had been betrayed once again, and ordered Bedivere a second time to throw Excalibur in the lake. This time, Bedivere told himself the King was too sick to know his own mind and that the sword should be kept as a relic for posterity. Again he returned to the King and once again Arthur ordered him to obey on pain of death. This time the knight obeyed, and as Excalibur fell into the water, an arm in a white sleeve rose from the waves, caught the sword by the hilt, and "brandishing him / Three times," withdrew it into the depths. When Bedivere reported this phenomenon, Arthur knew his will had been done.

The King knew his end was near and ordered Bedivere to help him to the lake's shore. Despite his pain, the King struggled to hurry, for he feared he would die before fulfilling his destiny. A dark barge appeared on the lake as they reached its shore, and they saw three queens robed in black, the same queens who had been Arthur's friends at court. They took him from Sir Bedivere and laid him on the barge, with cries of mourning.

Bedivere called to Arthur that there was no place left for him in the world without his king, and Arthur answered that the knight should retire to a life of prayer, for his sovereign and for the world that lay "bound by gold chains about the feet of God." As for himself, he declared he was on his way to the island of Avilion, where joy and spring reigned and he would be "healed of his wounds." Sir Bedivere watched the barge sail into the distance, and at last seemed to hear a faraway welcoming shout, as for a king "returning from his wars." From a high perch among the rocks, he thought he saw the King's barge leave the lake for the sea and then "vanish into light," as the sun rose and brought the new year. Bedivere kept the story in his heart, and told it to others when he was old.

CHARACTER ANALYSES

Arthur

Betrayed by all whom he had held dear, Arthur is beset by human fears that he has lost God also. Arthur is not a demi-god, but a mortal man, who has doubts about the worth of his own life and about his arrival at his heavenly destination, Avilion. He feels totally separated from other men, for they do not see reality as he sees it, and they have all betrayed his vision and his mission. In the dark night of his own doubt, helplessness and ruin, Arthur questions God and then remains satisfied with the answer given to him. His faith in Christ tells him that he will not die and that his life was not in vain.

Having secured the peace of his soul, Arthur struggles on to fulfill his duties down to the last moment of life. When Bedivere tries to deceive him, Arthur does not abandon his duty to dispose of Excalibur, but threatens Bedivere's life if that knight did not obey his ruler. His is conscious to the end of his kingly power, and of the obligation of his subjects to obey him. Despite his ideals and his personal gentleness, Arthur is a hero, not a monk.

He inflicts or threatens death even when dying himself. Knowing that his duty is to work the will of God in the real, fallen world of men, Arthur is able to act always with decision, promptness and total abandonment of self to duty.

Bedivere

As long as Bedivere believed that Arthur would ultimately conquer, he was utterly faithful and quick to encourage the King as they prepared for battle. Once it is clear that Arthur's death is near and that his kingship is destroyed, Bedivere is quick to betray his lord. He wants to save Arthur's sword because he cannot bear to give up that symbol of kingly power and triumph. Like so many others in the *Idylls*, Bedivere is strongly drawn to the tangible, temporal world, and will compromise his honor in order to keep the physical things which the world regards as beautiful and powerful. Once he has obeyed Arthur, Bedivere is purified, and he is allowed to witness the supernatural passing of the King. This sight gives him sustenance through all the bitter years of exile, loneliness and age.

Comment

The last battle assumes the larger dimensions of an ultimate sacrifice, a type of the Crucifixion itself. The battle is fought near the water which marked the beginning and the end of Arthur's career, and which is to be the site of his entry into heaven. The chilling mist which swept over the warrior during the battle has the supernatural quality of the storm at the death of Christ. The chill represents the death of both individuals and nature. Like his Savior in Gethsemane, Arthur groans in doubt and interior suffering over the coming struggle. His foes are like phantoms in the mist, and he feels himself a "King among the dead." His earthly kingdom has come to nothing and he is struck down by the most evil of his own followers. Like the crucified Christ, he lies among the three queens, his fair face marred with blood and dust. Also like his Lord, Arthur is taken into heaven, with the suggestion that he will come again to rule his kingdom.

The end of the Round Table is accomplished in "The Passing of Arthur." Friend fights friend in the all-encompassing mist, and all are struck down in that last battle which means the death of Arthur's vision for his country. The sea reclaims what it has given and the Round Table, "Which was an image of the mighty world," has "dissolved." Now the world is left to make what it will of the inspiration Arthur has given it, as it had to after the time of Christ.

ESSAY QUESTIONS AND ANSWERS

Question: What is the significance of the sun in "The Passing of Arthur"?

Answer: Arthur is often compared in the *Idylls* to the sun, either in its noonday brilliance or in its setting. His powers of creation, purity, and physical prowess suggest that he is a solar hero. The end of his kingly career occurs when the sun "Burn'd at his lowest in the rolling year," or at the winter solstice, and the barge bearing him to Avilion drifted from the sight of mortal men just before the first sunrise of the new year. Thus, the life of Arthur parallels both the yearly decline of the sun's influence occurring in winter, and the daily appearance and disappearance of the sun. At the height of the last battle, mist obscures the sun, and those who look to it as they cry to heaven are disappointed. Already, like Arthur, their sun is fading from their world, and is unable to save them from the death that must inevitably occur at the end of the old order. The new world, to which Arthur goes, has no snow or rain; it is subject to no changes such as men endure in this life. During the night which falls upon the world at Arthur's passing, prayer is the only human activity which will benefit mankind; the strong action which Arthur took in the world is to be superseded by prayer. Just as the sun signals the beginning of the day's labor, so night is the time for prayer and rest.

Question: What is the role of Excalibur in the idyll?

Answer: The solar hero is often the bearer of a sword, particularly of a sword which either burns or suggests flame. Arthur is no exception to this pattern. The jewelled Excalibur is the emblem of his kingly powers and the link which binds him to the temporal world where those powers are exercised. Once Bedivere has disposed of the sword, Arthur is free to abandon his kingdom and enter the next life. The flashing sword is received into the water from whence it came, just as the sun seems to sink into the sea at the day's end.

Throughout world mythology, the flaming sword also represents purification; it marks the cleavage between the purity of heaven and the suffering of earth. A sword is capable of inflicting death, and so serves as a force dividing this life from the next. Arthur bore his sword as he did his ideals, as a force for order and virtue in the temporal world. The sword is a masculine symbol, and throughout the *Idylls* Arthur's Excalibur accompanies him as a symbol of his own masculine power and authority. Excalibur, called "he" in the *Idylls*, embodies within itself the kingly and personal identity of Arthur. This identity is given into the hands of lesser men to do with as their conscience tells them. Just as the honor of Arthur is betrayed by his wife, his friend and his kingdom, so his authority (symbolized by Excalibur) is threatened by the deceit of Sir Bedivere. Ultimately, Sir Bedivere treats Excalibur as Arthur tells him to. In doing so, he honors the person of the King who has given the sign of kingly power into the knight's hands. As soon as Excalibur is gone, Arthur knows his end is at hand. The earthly, mortal personality that was King Arthur leaves the world of men with Excalibur; Arthur's soul belongs to the undying world of the spirit.

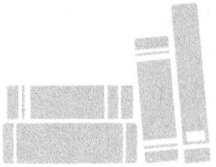

THE IDYLLS OF THE KING

THE LAST TOURNAMENT

PLOT ANALYSIS

In an eagle's nest, Lancelot had found a baby girl, which he brought to Arthur. The king gave her to his queen and she reared the baby lovingly until it died. The child had worn a ruby necklace when found, and Guinevere asked Arthur to make it a prize in a tournament to be held in the dead child's honor. A mutilated churl appeared to tell Arthur that a Red Knight, who had founded his own devil's version of the Round Table, had maimed him and sent him as a challenge to Arthur. Leaving Lancelot to judge the tournament, Arthur rode off to defeat his rival.

The tournament was won by Sir Tristram, lately returned from Brittany, where he had married Princess Isolt of the White Hands. She was pious and gentle, unlike the Isolt who was the wife of King Mark and Tristram's mistress. Dagonet, Arthur's devoted jester, taunts Tristram on his infidelity to the Round Table's code, and bitterly declares himself and Arthur both to be fools because they cling to the ideal.

Tristram set out to see Queen Isolt, hoping to placate her with the ruby necklace if she had heard of his marriage. On the way he dreamed that the two Isolts, one innocent and one guilty, pulled the necklace between them until the sinful queen won it and it made her hand red with blood.

While Tristram travelled to Isolt, Arthur battled the evil Red Knight. The Knight was overcome and his face trampled so that no one could learn his identity. Arthur's men burned the knight's tower and slaughtered all the lords and ladies. Though he had again secured his realm, Arthur's heart was heavy.

On his journey, Tristram met a woman weeping because her husband was gone. He advised her lightly not to spoil her looks with weeping lest her husband find her ugly and cease to love her. Later, when talking with Isolt, he refused to promise that he will love her when she has lost her beauty. King Mark was away on a hunt, but Isolt feared he would return and find them together. She objected to Tristram's marriage but hated her own husband so much that she took Tristram back regardless of his faithlessness. Tristram told his mistress not to worry about the other Isolt. Being meek and pious, his wife would probably become a nun. He refused to be bound to his mistress by any vow, for he believed that man's nature was too wild to be restrained by ideals. Isolt declared that Lancelot was far more courteous than he, but resigned herself to his faults. After a meal together, Tristram sang a love song to his lady and then offered her the necklace. Just as Tristram kissed her, Mark sprang from the shadows and cleaved his head in two.

That very night, Arthur returned from his war to find the loyal Dagonet weeping and saying that he could never again make his king smile. The queen's room was empty; Guinevere had left her husband.

CHARACTER ANALYSES

Dagonet

A reformed character through association with Arthur, Dagonet had once been filthy and foul-mouthed. Ironically, the loyal jester is now a truer knight to Arthur than the others in the court. He declares to Tristram that he has seen enough of the world's evil to convince him that the only salvation lies in being Arthur's fool. He admits the folly of trying to make good men out of sinners, but prefers to cling to the ideal regardless of the consequences. His loyalty is the standard by which the infidelity of all the other characters can be gauged.

Tristram

A man who lives completely to gratify his instincts, Tristram has no faith in the ideals of the King. He cares little for the hurt he causes others, assuming that if they are good, they will console themselves with religion, and if they are evil, they deserve no better treatment than he gives them. Isolt calls him a "wild beast" because he no longer allows himself to be motivated by the high ideals of the Round Table. Tristram justifies himself by declaring that the Round Table dream was over when Guinevere and Lancelot betrayed Arthur. He does not hold his mistress in high esteem, but betrays her easily and without remorse. His ideal is pagan, not Christian, and exalts the flesh over the spirit. It seems to Tristram that Arthur does not sufficiently recognize the demands of the natural man; indeed, Arthur does not come from the "flesh and blood / Of our old kings." As Arthur represents spirit, so Tristram represents flesh.

Isolt

Driven to a frenzy by her hatred of her ugly, evil husband, Isolt is dominated by a desire for love at no matter what cost. She begs Tristram to deceive her and tell her that he will love her forever, for she would rather hear a lie than believe herself ignobly loved. In her desperation, she taunts Tristram with his inferiority to Lancelot, but he cares nothing for her efforts at romantic idealism. Isolt is aware of her own great need for love, and is quick to assume that she needs her lover more than the other Isolt needs her husband. She is a woman of quick and absolute passions; when told by Mark that Tristram had married, she cried out that she would become a nun. Isolt demands a love so large and rich that it will give meaning to her entire life, but she is willing to settle for the careless Tristram, knowing that he is deceiving her. In her desire for romance and escape from a hated marriage, Isolt embraces fantasy and illusion as a way of life.

Arthur

As one would expect a Christian hero-king to be, Arthur is concerned even for the least of his people. He pities the orphan baby and asks his queen to take care of it as their own child. When the maimed churl comes to court, Arthur is filled with horror and pity. He sees that only an "evil beast" could have done such harm to a human being. Arthur feels that every man bears "heaven's image" in himself and is a person for whom Christ died. Yet in spite of his innocence, Arthur is not blind to faults. He is aware that the court has sunk to a lower level and his knights are in danger of becoming like wild beasts.

> Comment

Less than one-fifth of "The Last Tournament" is actually about the tournament, but the theme is the same throughout the poem: the decline of Arthur's knightly ideal. "The Last Tournament" is held in honor of "Dead Innocence," and is a nightmare celebration both of Guinevere's moral ruin and the Round Table's decline into a shadow of its former self. The child, a girl child whom Arthur gives to Guinevere, represents her own innocent virtue, which died early in their marriage instead of coming to maturity. The ruby necklace, a symbol of the child's innocence, ironically goes first into the hands of the guilty Guinevere and then into those of the guilty Isolt. Throughout the idyll, innocence and virtue are mocked by the ironic nature of events. Dagonet had been made a "mock-knight" of the Round Table, revealing the depths to which the ideal had fallen. Yet paradoxically, only "Sir Fool" mourned with Arthur when he found his queen had left him. The evil Red Knight, who had once been Arthur's knight, founded a Round Table of his own to counter the King's. His degradation is the sign of the ideal's decline and perversion, just as Tristram's illicit romance is a travesty of Lancelot's romance with Guinevere.

Nature itself plays the role of commentator on the action of the idyll. The "Tournament of the Dead Innocence" is held on a windy, rainy day in autumn, when the world is dying, like Arthur's court. The tournament knights are wet and muddy, an exterior condition which reflects their moral state. Lancelot, as ruler of the tournament, lets the laws of the tournament be broken freely and says nothing when a fallen knight openly curses the King and the dead child. As the year comes to its end, so does the glory of Arthur's court.

The spring promise and summer fruitfulness of Arthur's reign have faded to become the dreary disillusionment of autumn, just as the brilliant marriage of Arthur and Guinevere ends in sterility and betrayal. The "Tournament of Dead Innocence," conducted as it is with cynicism and curses, takes place in the mud and rains of autumn. The King's followers befoul themselves while trampling the Red Knight in the mud. Arthur's return from the wars to find his marriage shattered is also on a night of "death-dumb autumn-dripping gloom." All these images are related to the theme of decline and connect the idyll into a structural unity. As the cycle of Arthur's mission draws to a close, the cycle of the seasons unites with it to present a total picture of decay, moral as well as physical, individual as well as social.

ESSAY QUESTIONS AND ANSWERS

Question: Compare and contrast the attitudes of the characters in "The Last Tournament" toward romantic love.

Answer: There are two romantic triangles in the idyll, which are parallel in their destinies. Arthur, the betrayed husband of the first triangle is a paragon of virtue, and his rival, Lancelot, is courteous and charitable throughout the *Idylls*. King Mark, on the other hand, is ugly, evil and destructive. Tristram, Mark's betrayer, is selfish and cynical. The two queens, Isolt and Guinevere, are alike in their determination to have a romantic adventurous love affair to serve as an escape from prosaic reality, yet they differ in their motivation. Guinevere rejects Arthur because he is too good; Isolt rejects Mark because he is too evil.

Arthur and Lancelot both base their ideal of romantic love for Guinevere on respect for her person and the belief that their earthly passion is a symbol of a higher, spiritual love which will be fulfilled completely only in the next life. Tristram feels that the ugly, profane world he sees around him is not his fault and that he may as well enjoy the pleasures available to him. He and Mark reveal by their attitudes the nature of earthly love once it is stripped of all its divine and human inspiration and reduced to mere lust. They represent the "beast," or unregenerate humanity, which will not permit Arthur to act as its conscience and raise it to a higher level.

Question: How are the tournament and Arthur's war against the Red Knight bound together in the structure of the idyll?

Answer: Both the tournament and the war are linked by a single **theme**: the decay of the chivalric ideal. Arthur is betrayed on all sides by fallen knighthood. The Red Knight was once the King's man, but has turned against his former vows. While Arthur battles this renegade, he must leave the judgment of the joust to Lancelot, also a betrayer. The tournament is peopled by craven, blasphemous knights and is won by the cynical Tristram. Both in the tournament and in the war, Arthur's ideal is battered until it is unrecognizable, like the face of the Red Knight whom Arthur's knights savagely mutilate. Beset by evil knights at home and abroad, betrayed by his friend and first lieutenant, Arthur is the victim of the men he hoped to change. We are shifted back and forth between the scenes of battle, serious and mock, so that the poet's intention becomes unmistakable: to reveal the parallel decline of Arthur's realm in war and peace.

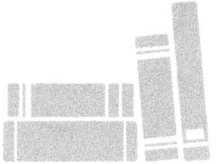

THE IDYLLS OF THE KING

GARETH AND LYNETTE

PLOT ANALYSIS

Gareth, the youngest son of Queen Bellicent, was eager to follow his two older brothers to Arthur's court, but Bellicent wanted to keep him safely with her. He pleaded with her so much, that at last she consented to let him go, on the condition that he serve incognito as a kitchen boy at Arthur's court. To her surprise, he sets off gladly, accepting her challenge, leaving her alone with her husband, Lot. Arthur had defeated Lot's rebellion years before, but had given him back his land. This defeat had caused Lot to sink into silent despondency.

With two companions, Gareth arrived at Camelot, after first having a vision of a fairy city with a mysterious seer who warned them of the purity necessary to serve Arthur. Gareth entered the joyful court, where Arthur was granting boons to his people, both friends and enemies, as they approached him. The only boon he would not grant was to the evil King Mark, who wished to become a knight of the Round Table. The request of Gareth to become a kitchen boy was granted, and the surly Sir Kay was given charge of him. Though Sir Kay treated him rudely, Gareth was unfailingly courteous toward him and toward his fellow kitchen servants. Lancelot suspected that Gareth was of noble birth and was kind to him. After a month, Bellicent relented and released her son from his promise. Gareth revealed himself to Arthur and was promised a quest.

Lynette, a lady from a beleaguered castle, came to court to complain to Arthur that the land was not yet pacified, and that her sister, Lyonors, was under siege by four evil suitors. Her tower, the Castle Perilous, was surrounded by a river with three loops and three crossings, each guarded by a knight; and the castle itself was being attacked by the most powerful of the four knights. Lynette called for Sir Lancelot to come and aid her sister, but to her dismay, Arthur sent Gareth. Lynette ran from the court, but Gareth followed her, outfitted with Arthur's horse. He, in turn, was followed by Lancelot, whom Arthur had sent to watch over the fledgling knight from afar, over Sir Kay's protests.

When Gareth caught up with Lynette, she held her nose and greeted him with mockery. Gareth met her abuse with courtesy, intent upon his duty at all costs. He rescued a baron who was about to be killed by thieves, but Lynette would not consider this a sufficient proof of his prowess. Next he battled Sir Morningstar or "day," defeated him, and sent him back to Arthur without his shield. Lynette relented only for a moment during the battle, but again was turned against Gareth by the thought of his lowly social position. Next Gareth fought the powerful knight, "Noonday Sun," and won when his enemy's horse slipped. Lynette saw little merit in this victory, and further accused Gareth of lacking a noble's sensitivity to beauty and emotional depth. Gareth vanquished the old knight "Evening star" after his greatest struggle, and Lynette at last commended him and allowed him to ride at her side.

As they rested in a cave, Lynette showed him the allegory of the knights against whom he fought engraved in stone, pursuing the soul who fled to that cave for safety. Lancelot then caught up with them and briefly jousted with Gareth, whom he did not recognize. The exhausted Gareth was overthrown, to Lynette's annoyance. When Lancelot learned Gareth's identity, he offered to teach him the tricks he would need to overcome his last foe, but Gareth refused. He borrowed Lancelot's shield, and over Lynette's concerned protests, went off to fight Death, the last of the knights, instead of allowing Lancelot to take his place. When Gareth cleaved open the head of the dreaded, dark figure of death, a boy's head appeared from it, to the merriment of all. One tale had it that Gareth then married the rescued Lady Lyonors, but another declared that he wed Lynette.

CHARACTER ANALYSES

Gareth

While he is still at his parents' castle, Gareth is symbolized by a waterfall carrying away the knightly pine. Arthur is symbolized as the sun, while Gareth is his servant, the eagle who falls upon "all things base." He is the type of the "good servant," utterly faithful to his master's will, utterly truthful in the execution of that will amidst the snares and impurities of the world.

Bellicent

Once convinced of Arthur's divine claims, Bellicent has been swayed by her emotions to deny these claims in order to keep Gareth with her. Since her husband and older sons can no longer serve as company for her, she is selfishly determined to prevent

Gareth from fulfilling his destiny, and wants to keep him forever at her side. Again her emotions rule her, in contrast to the disposition of Gareth, who never allows himself to be dominated by emotion in the face of duty.

Lynette

A proud young woman of great family, Lynette is described as having fierce eyes and a slender, tilted nose. She finds it impossible to give up her false notions about reality, until Gareth proves to her that appearance does not make the man. Once she sees clearly, however, her nature is proved to be a tender, feminine one, as is illustrated by her lyrical blessing over Gareth, asleep in the cave after his victory.

Comment

Early in the poem, Gareth declares his intention to be an arm of King Arthur's, serving the king in the battle against disorder and impurity. Like Galahad is to be, Gareth is a pure youth, raised by a woman in isolation from the affairs of warring men, and thus he represents innocence. His aim is twofold, to follow Christ and Arthur. To fulfill his manhood, he must leave the smothering ministrations of his mother. When he joins the company of another woman, Lynette, it is necessary to prove himself a man in order to be accepted, a relationship directly opposite to the one he enjoyed with his mother.

Gareth's vision of the fairy city outside time is actually a glimpse of the ideal order being built up by Arthur, but destined never to be realized fully except in heaven. By becoming Arthur's servant, Gareth enters into the "living gateway" of the city, and is part of the heavenly kingdom. This is the first clear suggestion in the poem that all Gareth will encounter is not exactly what it seems, and that Gareth himself will not be recognized by others for what he is. Sir Kay and Lynette, like Guinevere in "The Coming of Arthur," depend upon the outward signs of status for determining the worth of a man. Arthur, Lancelot and the baron Gareth rescued are able to perceive the nobility of the inward man; Arthur approves of the lowly Gareth, but rejects the evil King Mark.

In doing battle against the four knights, Gareth fights those ills that confront every man: the trials of the time of youth, the trials of maturity, and the trials of old age culminating in death. By using Arthur's horse and acting in Arthur's name, Gareth assumes something of Arthur's ideal nature. He is thus representative of all men in conflict with the universal human enemies. Like Arthur, Gareth bases his life on honesty and fidelity to duty, even when he is mocked for doing so. His origins are doubted by Kay and Lynette, just as Arthur's origins were questioned. For Gareth, words mean little; he is content to depend upon deeds for his reputation, and it is by his deeds that Gareth judges Arthur worthy of being served.

In overcoming the first knight, Morning-Star, Gareth also overcomes the perils of youth, just as he overcame the temptation to stay with his mother, forever a child, and seeks manhood at Arthur's court. As he subdues the knights who represent the struggles of manhood and old age, he fights more painfully, almost overcome by the forces of despair within himself.

Lynette reveals the nature of the combat when she describes to Gareth the allegory on the stone: it is the "War of Time" against the soul of man. She herself is linked with these knights, and gives religious adoration to the heavenly, ideal symbols, which the knights can only play at imitating. She is thankful to the Sun and the Morning and Evening Stars, when the knights are vanquished; for in his allegorical battle, Gareth fights for Lynette's freedom as well as everyman's. When the knights are beaten, so too is Lynette's proud soul.

The final victory, over death itself, proves that the horrible knight was only a deceiver after all. In reality, he was different from his appearance, being only a "blooming boy." Gareth has succeeded in unmasking the last liar. The truth which he has served has freed him from fear, and he is able to see that death only passes into new life. A menacing note is sounded, however, despite the general rejoicing at the poem's end. The evil knights' real target is revealed to be Arthur himself, the representative of humanity striving for the ideal.

ESSAY QUESTIONS AND ANSWERS

Question: What is the nature of reality in the world of "Gareth and Lynette"? How do false ideas about reality confuse some of the characters until the end of the poem?

Answer: In terms of ultimate worth and power, the ideal world toward which Arthur aims dominates the narrative. Yet this reality-in-the making is still shadowy and mysterious to the eyes of men. Even Gareth sees the phantom city only as in a dream. Reality, as men can know it here and now, consists primarily in the accomplishment of one's duty to persevere in faith and in service to the king (both to Christ and to Arthur). Only in this way can the ideal be made to correspond to reality as we recognize it. Men without spiritual vision doubt Arthur's claims and they likewise are unable to understand the double nature of reality. They see only the apparent real world, with its pomps and labels, not the spiritual reality which transfigures it from within. Kay is annoyed with Lancelot for suggesting that Gareth is not the kitchen boy he seems to be, and complains that it is foolish to talk of mystery. Failure to understand that appearance and reality must inevitably be mixed in this world means that the character who thus fails cannot achieve the wisdom necessary for right judgment. Faith, obedience, fidelity to duty, and loving gratitude are the means to winning the wisdom needed to sort the false appearances from interior realities.

Question: What are the indications in the poem that Arthur is threatened by forces outside and within Camelot? How do these forces cause the atmosphere of the court to be different from what it was in the first idyll?

Answer: While Arthur is still surrounded by devoted men and pure women, his court does not have the same triumphant atmosphere that we sense at the end of "The Coming of Arthur." The wicked King Mark of Cornwall is attempting to worm his way into the fellowship of the Round Table. Though his corrupting influence is rejected, his representative and cousin, Tristram, is one of the company, and his presence bodes ill for the future of Camelot. The ignominious blank shield of the evil Modred, Gareth's older brother, suggests that all Arthur's knights are not as devoted to the ideal as they might appear. Sir Kay's unchivalrous attitude toward those of lower status than he reveals another side to the court of Arthur, at which perfect justice might be expected. A widow of a baron slain by Arthur in a rebellion claims justice at Arthur's hands and receives it, though she still admits to being the king's enemy. Despite all the efforts of Arthur's knights, the old human enemies of suffering and death still prowl the land, and keep the ideal from becoming a complete reality. These enemies lie in wait for Arthur as for all heroes, and threaten both him and Camelot with extinction, even when Camelot is secure to all appearances.

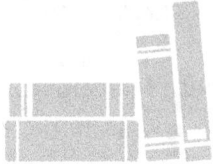

THE IDYLLS OF THE KING

BALIN AND BALAN

PLOT ANALYSIS

Having just sent a mission to collect tribute from the faithless King Pellam, Arthur went alone to do battle with two strange knights, who had been in the forest near Camelot, challenging all who came near them. Arthur overcame them, and learned from Balin that he had been banished for three years from Arthur's court by the king's own command. Balin had injured a servant of Arthur's in anger, and now hoped that his bravery in challenging all who passed him in the forest would make Arthur want to take him back. Balan, his brother, had accompanied Balin, who needed constant watching because of his insane rages. The two brothers were forgiven and welcomed back by Arthur.

The embassy to King Pellam returned, declaring that Pellam was trying to rival Arthur in holiness by collecting relics, fasting excessively, separating himself from his wife, and handing over the administration of his realm to his evil heir, Garlon, who refused to pay the tribute due Arthur. The ambassadors also reported that one of their number had been killed by a demon who dwelled in a cave in Garlon's woods. Balan left to fight the demon, warning Balin not to disgrace the Round Table by going back to his previous mad moods.

Balin schooled himself in virtue, copying Lancelot above all the knights at court, especially Lancelot's devotion to the Queen. Despairing at his lack of gentility, Balin begged for and received the right to wear Guinevere's royal device on his shield, so that from it he might learn mildness and courtesy. For a time he made progress, but his baser urges continually reminded him that he was not fit for Camelot. In this agonized frame of mind, Balin overheard an intimate and compromising conversation between Lancelot and Guinevere. Unable to trust his estimate of the lovers' encounter, Balin became confused, and attributed his interpretation of the queen's relationship with the King's best knight to his own baseness. Without asking the king's permission, Balin rushed off after Balan to do battle with the demon.

After an unsuccessful brush with the demon of the woods, Balin arrived at the court of King Pellam, where Garlon mocked him for wearing the device of the impure Guinevere on his shield. One day of such mockery was all Balin could bear. In a rage, he killed Garlon, making his escape by hurling at his pursuers the Sacred Lance from the Holy Land. Once again in the woods, Balin hung the shield on a branch, convinced he had shamed it by his murderous rage and did not deserve to carry it any longer.

Vivien, a "damsel-errant" from the court of the evil King Mark, rode by, singing of the victory she hoped the sun-worshipping heathen would win over the Cross and the King. Vivien asked Balin to guide her to Arthur's court, for she declared she fled from the unwanted attentions of a suitor. Balin refused, saying he was too savage to face the pure

Guinevere again. Lying easily, Vivien declared that her squire had seen Lancelot and Guinevere embrace and that Balin had no reason to feel himself inferior to such hypocrites. Balin was driven into a frenzy by her words, which he was sure were true, having seen the guilty couple in a questionable situation himself. He trampled the shield with its crown and uttered the cries of a madman. Hearing them, Balan who was in hiding nearby waiting for the demon, rushed out and attacked Balin. With the Holy Lance, the latter mortally wounded Balan, while Balin's own horse reeled and fell upon him, crushing him to the point of death. Vivien, assuming Balin had been a jealous rival of Lancelot's, went on to Camelot with her adoring young squire. Balin and Balan revived only long enough to recognize each other, and then died in each other's arms.

CHARACTER ANALYSES

Balin

Judged by Arthur to be a man of complete honesty, Balin has as his chief virtue an utterly humble, truthful view of himself. In his humility, he judges himself harshly for his violent passions and the acts that follow them. He recognizes worth in others, just as he recognizes evil in himself, and gives absolute fidelity to those he believes are worthy of trust. His sins are not calculated ones, but are committed suddenly in a fit of passion, and are bitterly repented.

Balan

Though innocent himself, Balan shares his brother's exile, and deeply desires to be his brother's keeper. Only his higher loyalty to Arthur causes him to leave his brother's side temporarily, to the ruin of them both. Like Balin, he is quick to act for justice; Balan is the first of the knights to volunteer against the demon. Yet he does not share his brothers's ungovernable fury against evil; Balan prudently ignores Garlon's mockery, knowing that Garlon is angry about the tribute.

Pellam

Once an irreligious, rebel king, Pellam saw that Arthur prospered by espousing Christ, and determined to outshine the other king in devotion to God. Instead of fulfilling his vocation as a good king, he abandons his responsibilities and lives the life of a monk. He selfishly puts his own desires ahead of the kingdom's needs. His hypocrisy and weakness contrast unfavorably with the doomed Balin's courage and self-knowledge.

Vivien

A whole-hearted servant of this world in its seamier aspects, Vivien professes a set of values consistent with her worldliness. She is the enemy of asceticism, and conspires with Garlon against the wishes of the old king Pellam. Equally, she despises the honor of the Round Table and Arthur's mission to bring heavenly ideals into the service of humanity. It is she whose lies bring the first bitter harvest of Lancelot's and Guinevere's betrayal of Arthur. She is unconcerned for the fate of Balin and Balan after their battle, which she caused by her lies. Despite her own wickedness, she dares to accuse Guinevere of evil. Unlike the humble Balin, Vivien has no concern for the defects in her own character and no remorse for her wicked deeds.

Comment

From the time we first encounter Balin and Balan by a fountain, they operate with the force of a single personality. They even answer Arthur with one voice when he addresses them, and they enter combat together. Balin cannot be left behind by his guiding spirit, Balan, for long. After his confusion at the court, he follows, perhaps unconsciously, the footsteps of Balan to the castle of King Pellam. In the end, the two fall in battle at the same moment, having destroyed one another. Clearly, they are meant to represent the two sides of human personality, which must function together as a creative unit. Balin is the rough, passionate, violent aspect of character, while Balan is the idealistic, gentle, prudent one. They can survive only when the latter controls the former, that is, when soul controls body. Their separation and subsequent failure to recognize one another results in mutual disaster. Their problem is a central theme of the *Idylls* as a whole, and their failure to solve the problem is a harbinger of doom for the court which they serve. The fact that Vivien participates in their ruin indicates that Arthur's ideals are being threatened by forces outside his realm as well as by those within the court itself.

Another pair of characters in the idyll suffers from the same kind of duality which afflicts Balin and Balan: Pellam and Gorlon. Pellam cuts himself off from the concerns of the body, even those concerns which men like Arthur are able to sanctify by their high, spiritual ideals. He abdicates from the world, leaving his representative, Gorlon, to take his place. In effect, he splits his nature in two, with one half dwelling in the chapel among the relics, and the other half free to do unrestrained evil in the world of men. Gorlon is said to have learned magic, and to be the invisible demon of the woods. He is the friend of the destructive Vivien, who has been driven off by the virtuous Pellam because she is female and might pollute the castle. Having set aside the moderating influence of women by separating himself from his good wife, Pellam has left himself vulnerable to failure in this world and the next. Gorlon is the alter-ego of Pellam himself, and prowls like a phantom or wild beast in the lawless forests, unchecked by any restraints of conscience.

The forests in which the wild Balin and Gorlon wander are part of the waste land which threatens Arthur's mission and the order of the court. The failure of Balin and Balan to integrate themselves as one successful personality, contrasts with the previous triumph of Geraint in winning maturity and perfect manhood. The fall of Balin and Balan begins a new and darker section of the *Idylls*, in which man is to fail woman (Lancelot and Elaine) and woman is to fail man (Merlin and Vivien, Guinevere). Balin himself is betrayed and undone as Arthur is to be, by the illicit love of Guinevere for Lancelot. Woman cannot save man in "Balin and Balan"; the old essential, fundamental unity of man and women is broken, and only failure can result when this occurs.

ESSAY QUESTIONS AND ANSWERS

Question: How does violence within man parallel violence that takes place in the world around him in "Balin and Balan"?

Answer: While confessing his faults to King Arthur, Balan sees and admits that his violent deeds had not been merely outer ones. He would also have done violence within himself, if it had not been for his better self, Balan. Throughout the idyll, Balan suffers a tumult of confusion in his soul, doubting himself and those around him, a situation which parallels the marked unevenness of his conduct and his relationship with others. He vows to serve Arthur, but disobeys him to follow Balan; he vows to serve Guinevere, but in a rage stamps upon her symbol. With good reason does Balin desire to do battle with the demon of the woods so that he might allay the devil within himself. Like every faithful knight of Arthur's court, he is aware that only in outward, noble action will he achieve the nobility of soul he so desires. Pellam fails to see this connection of spirituality with deeds in the world outside the soul. All that Pellam can see when Gorlon has been killed is that Balin defiles the Holy Lance "with earthly uses." He does not see the essential truth: that the Lance, like the Grail and all possessions of the spirit, is meant to be used in the redemption of the earth.

Question: What is the role of the shield in "Balin and Balan"?

Answer: Regardless of her conduct as an individual, Guinevere stands for the gentleness, nobility and innocence of woman. This is especially so because Guinevere is the wife of Arthur, the intended vessel of honor, justice and virtue with which Arthur desires to fill the world at large. In her union with Arthur, Guinevere represents mankind in its noblest, most creative aspect. When Balin desires to bear her device upon his shield, he craves also all those virtues which her position entitles her to represent. Both Balin and Balan strive for the good as long as they are subject to the shield and the sign upon it. It is only when Balin puts off the shield and tramples on it that he brings about his ruin. Without that shield, Balin is merely a savage, as are all men without the mark of civilization and gentility upon them. Balan, who continues till the end to believe in Guinevere and all she represents, cannot recognize his own brother as a man without the shield, but thinks him a demon instead. The ideal is what saves men; even though individuals may fail it, each man has the obligation to trust it until death.

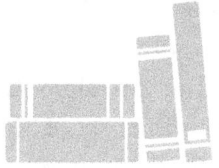

OTHER POEMS

THE PALACE OF ART

COMPOSITION

There were several influences at work upon Tennyson when he conceived the idea for "The Palace of Art." At Cambridge he had discussed the relationship of life to art with a friend, R. C. Trench (later Archbishop Trench). Trench had said, "Tennyson, we cannot live in art." Tennyson evidently gave this much thought, and it is certain that he talked the problem over with his friend Arthur Hallam. It may have been to Hallam or Trench that the poem "To -----", which accompanied "The Palace of Art," was dedicated. Hallam wrote Tennyson a letter, dated July 26, 1831, in which he discusses the matter. First he compares his own mind to that of the poet, remarking that while Tennyson is totally absorbed by his art, Hallam himself must be open to many other influences. He quotes Tennyson as saying, "Alas for me! I have more of the beautiful than the good!" Hallam sympathizes with this position, calling it the poet's God-given genius, but he is nevertheless glad that Tennyson recognizes the pitfalls inherent in the "art-for-art's-sake" philosophy.

Tennyson resolved the problem to his own satisfaction apparently, for throughout the rest of his career he left no doubt that he chose Wisdom over artistic Beauty as the supreme human goal. He said, "'The Palace of Art' is the embodiment of my own belief that the God-like life is with man and for man..." By temperament, Tennyson was a lyrical poet, with a particular gift for natural description, and only a secondary interest in theology, science and ethics. The crucial decision of his life was to put aside, once and for all, the mere exercise of lyric talent for the sake of an attempted synthesis of Truth and Beauty. Critics have long debated whether or not he aimed too high and was thereby false to his particular genius.

The poem was written when Tennyson was only twenty-three, yet it bears the marks of his maturing style upon it. "The Palace of Art" appeared in Tennyson's second volume of verse, published in December, 1832, by Moxon. It was one of thirty poems, greatly varying in style and subject. Even before its publication, "The Palace of Art" had circulated among Tennyson's friends, one of whom already knew the work by heart. It is a poem of 296 lines, with stanzas of four lines each, rhyming according to an A B A B pattern. The first line and the third line of each **stanza** are five-beat or **pentameter** lines, the second is four-beat or **tetrameter**, while the fourth line is three-beat or trimeter.

CRITICAL OPINION

When the volume was published, only the "Apostles" at Cambridge approved of its contents. The public thought the poems "affected and obscure," while the literary critics almost universally disliked and mocked them. One critic went so far as to suggest that Tennyson belonged in a madhouse. By 1835, when an approving review by John Stuart Mill appeared, only 300 of the original 800 copies had been sold. Later critical opinion has somewhat restored the volume's reputation, at least in the case of single works like "The Palace of Art." This poem is now regarded generally as a competent and occasionally brilliant piece, though opinion persists that the main body of the poem, which celebrates Art's splendid isolation, usurps too much of the poet's attention. This is considered a serious fault because the end of the poem indicates that art is less important to man's life than truth.

PLOT ANALYSIS

The poet describes the situation of his soul in allegorical terms. The soul dwells in a "pleasure-house," which allows it to enjoy itself in solitude. The palace is then described. The foundation is a smooth rock platform, rising suddenly into the light out of a grassy meadow. The walls of rock below the palace are smooth, so that no one can scale them and disturb the soul. Around the palace there are four square courtyards, and these hold four fountains, whose waters eventually pour in a cataract down the mountain to the meadows below. On the heights around the palace are statues, reaching up to heaven with incense poured from a "golden cup."

The soul passes from "room to room," down the many echoing corridors of its palace, enjoying the mirror of nature which exists within its walls: the peaceful beach, the stormy ocean, a river flowing through the plains, reapers at the harvest, snow-capped mountains, and a quiet English household. All these are designed with perfect fidelity to the model as it exists in the real world below.

The palace is peopled with many figures. They represent the mythologies of all Aryan peoples and the great authors of the past: Dante, Milton and Homer. Other subjects are also represented: the people at their daily tasks, the kings who rule them, the heroes who rise above the level of the common man. Beyond all these, however, the soul (now referred to in the poem simply as "she") takes her place on the throne. The great tower bells, which ring by themselves, toll as she sings her songs. Plato and Francis Bacon, the ancient and the modern representatives of philosophy, smile upon her. As she sings, she rejoices in her power over nature and the senses, remote from the sufferings and triumphs of mankind. She acknowledges as gods only the wise figures of the past that dwell with her. From afar the soul watches the "swine" on the plains below, seeing them as creatures of a lower order than her own; and she also regards their religion and morality as inferior to her god-like state, in which creeds are insignificant.

Despite the sufferings of men, the soul continues to enjoy her throne and powers for three years. In the fourth year, however, she experiences a heaven-sent despair and is unable to overcome her confusion. Like the Biblical King Belshazzar, the soul is spoken to by handwriting on the wall, which tells her that her kingdom is at an end. Her solitude becomes hateful to her, and her mood varies between dread and complacency, for she still recognizes the grandeur of her possession. Yet the soul is now haunted by dark ghosts from the unexplored parts of her palace. She stumbles upon dead bodies that remind her of her own mortality, and finally sees herself as a rootless being, unattached to the forward movement of men and events in the outside world.

In her pride, the soul fights against her sense of isolation and exile from God and man. Life and death, time and eternity are equally dreadful to her. Her palace has become a tomb; the sounds outside it can no longer be determined because the mind has grown dull to human associations. In desperation, she cries out for salvation from sin and death. At the end of her fourth year in the palace, she casts aside her kingly garments and begs for a "cottage in the vale" in which she can "mourn and pray." However, she desires to leave the palace intact so that she may come back purified with companions at a later time.

Comment

"The Palace of Art" represents Tennyson's mature grappling with the alternatives available to the poet in his own time. The romantic poets, with their insistence on Beauty, had come and gone. The Victorian Age demanded morality and ideals as well as Beauty. Tennyson had to decide whether he would adopt the standards of his own age or of the previous generation of poets. Hallam, as we have seen, encouraged a non-romantic approach to art, and this influence no doubt proved a potent one in the development of Tennyson's poetic attitudes. Tennyson himself says of "The Palace of Art" that it "represents allegorically the condition of a mind which, in the love of beauty and the triumphant consciousness of knowledge, and intellectual supremacy, in the intense enjoyment of its own power and glory, has lost sight of its relation to man and God." Tennyson found it necessary to form a position on the Goethean themes then sweeping the Continent and England. For Goethe's *Faust*, human ambition, curiosity and secular achievement were sufficient to engage the full energies of man. This point of view Tennyson explores thoroughly in "The Palace of Art," and ultimately rejects. Throughout his poems, he maintains an attitude consistent with this position, though it was formulated as early as twenty-three years of age. This represents a continuity of intellectual commitment highly unusual in literary history.

The first condition of the soul in "The Palace of Art" is blissful confidence in its self-sufficiency and power. The image of height is used frequently in the early part of the poem, emphasizing the proud, egotistical attitude of the soul in its first moments of glory. The soul thinks of itself as a king, but a king remote from its subjects. The static immobility of such a position is hinted at (but not explored until the latter half of the poem) by the reference to the apparently motionless shadow of Saturn which is visible on its rings. The number four is prominent also, and is used to suggest completeness within a limited area. At first this area allows the soul all the freedom it desires, but later the restricted area is felt to be too small, and the palace's limitations cause the soul to despair.

The poet occupies a position between heaven and earth; he looks down at the plains below, and all around him incense ascends to heaven. The water that flows from around his palace to the land beneath it represents the almost involuntary overflow of the poet's talents on mankind. The incense which rises perpetually from the palace to heaven is the poet's offering to God. Contemplating all this grandeur, the soul expands in pride, delighted that simple mortals are dazzled by his genius. It lives independent of time, for its incense rises unfailingly, whether the day begins or ends. Later in the poem, it becomes clear that this independence of time and human progress is not an unmixed blessing.

As the soul travels in its palace, we are told that the rooms it visits stand for the varying sources of the poet's inspiration. Nature is given first place in this long roll-call of the subjects for poetic treatment. Next in significance are the mythologies which furnish the poet with his heroes: the Christian story, represented by the Virgin Mother of Jesus and the Virgin Saint Cecilia, Moslem belief by the Houris of Paradise, English legend by King Arthur, Roman mythology by King Numa the Law-Giver, Hindu mythology by Cama the God of Love, and Greek legend by Europa and Ganymede. All these scenes and characters exist in the poet's imagination in perfect fidelity to the original, for Tennyson felt that accuracy was one of the poet's supreme responsibilities.

The portraits hanging close to the soul's own throne are those of great literary men and philosophers, especially the ancient idealist, Plato, and the "modern" pragmatist, Francis Bacon. Above them, in a scene reminiscent of Jacob's Ladder, angels come and go between the soul and God. The floor of the throne room, its foundation, is "mosaic," and suggests that the basis of the soul's imaginative activity is the tradition of literary and religious man through the ages. This stanza on the mosaic floor replaces a complex one in an earlier version, in which many names of Hebrew prophets and of Renaissance and classical figures appear. In the interests of simplicity, Tennyson evidently decided to reduce this catalogue to the "mosaic" of general civilized tradition. It is briefly suggested in 11. 165-8 that the wise men surrounding the soul are clearly linked to human progress, in contrast to the proud soul in its lonely palace. That the soul is not altogether its own master is suggested in lines 130 and 158, where the bells ring mysteriously of themselves. Bells in Tennyson's poetry often indicate spiritual communication, and here they seem to refer to the soul's ultimate dependence for inspiration upon God.

Once enthroned, the soul proceeds to examine its condition. Like the statue of Memnon in Egypt, which sang in answer to the dawn's light, the soul pours forth melodies. She rejoices simply in her existence and her powers, without regard for their responsible use, for she feels responsible to no one. She takes a neutral position with regard to human suffering, and feels no solidarity with the rest of mankind or its concerns. As night comes, the soul lights its palace so brilliantly as to "mimic heaven," for she still believes herself capable of unaided divinity. Her gods are those great men surrounding her, and she acknowledges no need for salvation, as the common run of humanity requires. To her, human beings are mere swine, and their fate is to be viewed with callous objectivity by such elevated beings as herself. The soul is thus convinced that she alone is immortal, though all human beings perish like animals. She takes what she chooses from civilization, but thinks herself and her opinions superior to any religious doctrines.

After her three years of prosperity, the soul, like Herod, fell because she would not acknowledge herself a sinful human creature before almighty God. Through God-given suffering and despair at her own limitations, the pride of the poet is overcome. All the soul can fall back on is the continuity of her own development; from her "first memory" in childhood, her identity has been the same even in its imaginative growth. The ghosts in the unconscious mind of every man now haunt the isolated soul, and stir up doubts of her glory. These ghosts are the phantoms of sin from which no man can honestly excuse himself. The corpses that the soul comes upon are vivid symbols of her own inevitable death.

Confronting the fact that she must some day die, the soul is finally able to understand that she has never truly lived. While the evolutionary future of man, with its dimly-seen utopian future, proceeds in the real world of human beings and events, the soul is alone in its backwater. She is like a star which holds itself aloof from the harmonious intermovements ordained by

God for all the heavenly bodies. In her pride, the soul at first rejects this vision of her inadequacies, crying that she would not listen to the voice of sanity. Tennyson depicts the world of men without faith in his description of the soul sunk in her stubborn despair: such men find no comfort in contemplating this life or the next.

Gradually, the links with the outside world dissolve, leaving the soul as though in a tomb, an ironic destiny for the proud one who had established her own "new land." Again, the shock brought about by the prospect of death arouses the soul to repent its sin and cry out for salvation. Her penance is to be performed in humble circumstances, in union with the vast lot of human kind. The palace of imagination is not destroyed, for it is not evil of itself; only the soul that dwells in it makes it good or evil. Only the artist purified by suffering and sympathy with other men can safely dwell in this palace, and even he must not enter it unless he shares its joys with others.

ESSAY QUESTIONS AND ANSWERS

Question: How does Tennyson conceive "the whole man"?

Answer: A man who is a successful and complete human being, as well as a successful poet, must not live through his imagination alone. He must possess the gift of seeing himself as he is. The imaginative powers he possesses are immense, and give him a resemblance to the angels, but they must not make him proud. God is able to see the "abysmal deeps of personality," and man must learn to see them in himself, as it were with the eyes of God. Within the animal depths of man are obscure urges to sin and destruction, combatting the soul's longing for beauty and order. These "deeps" must be honestly faced, and man requires

God's help in order to protect himself from them. He must not attempt to shut out love from his philosophy, or think that the abstract contemplation of beauty is enough to sustain his soul. In the prologue to "The Palace of Art," Tennyson insists that beauty, virtue and knowledge must co-exist in every complete individual. It is primarily through the experience of human life, with its sufferings and the confrontation of inevitable death, that this ideal condition of integrity or "wholeness" is achieved.

Question: According to "The Palace of Art," what is the role of the artist in society?

Answer: Tennyson is highly critical of the point of view, held by artists like the Roman Lucretius, that the artist ought to hold himself aloof from the society in which he lives. Instead of dropping his jewels of beauty indifferently to the inferior beings beneath him, the artist must consider himself solidly one with the rest of the human race. He should live simply, not royally, and share the condition of mankind so that he can transform it properly into meaningful art. The concerns that occupy his mind should be those common to all men, not esoteric subjects. He must not only live with others, he must share the palace of his imagination with others also. The artist needs other men in order to fulfill his vocation, just as others need him to teach them how to appreciate beauty. Together, they participate in the building of the ideal world that is to come in the distant future.

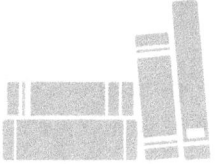

OTHER POEMS

IN MEMORIAM

COMPOSITION

Shortly after having returned from Scotland on a brief trip, Tennyson received a letter from Arthur Hallam, who was accompanying his father, the historian Henry Hallam, on a continental tour. This letter, written on September 6, 1833, was the last one Tennyson was destined to receive from his closest friend. Several days after its composition, Hallam was stricken with a slight fever. His father left him resting in their Vienna hotel room for a short time, and returned to find his son dead of a burst blood vessel. The news of Hallam's death rocked Tennyson's religious faith and permanently changed his life. He was already in a state of gloom because of the harsh reviews of his 1832 volume, and he relied deeply on Hallam's confidence in his genius. Hallam's own brilliance and charm made his early death difficult to reconcile with the orthodox concept of an all-good God. Tennyson's struggles with doubt and despair were given a focus by the death of Hallam, though the poet's life even before this event had been marked by melancholy introversion. The transmutation of personal grief into poetry took Tennyson seventeen years to accomplish, and it was not until 1850 that *In*

Memoriam was privately published. Critics attacked it at first, but the general public was so overwhelmingly approving, that criticism became muted and finally ceased altogether. It was said that Prince Albert decided to grant Tennyson the Laureateship on the basis of "In Memoriam." In any case, the poem spoke to Victorian England in a penetrating and inspiring voice, and dealt with matters particularly relevant to the soul of that age.

FORM AND METER

Though the form used by Tennyson for his **stanzas** had been used by Sir Philip Sidney and Ben Jonson, it is now known as the "In Memoriam" **stanza**, a tribute to the power and stature of the poem in the eyes of literary historians. Each **stanza** has four eight-syllable (octosyllabic) lines, with the **rhyme** scheme A B B A. The **stanzas** are grouped into sections of varying length, numbering 131 in all, plus the 11-stanza Proem or Prologue. Initially, Tennyson says in his *Memoir*, "I did not write them with any view of weaving them into a whole, or for publication, until I found I had written so many." The overall impression of the poem is not one of artfully constructed, logical sequence or pattern, but of a psychological unity, involving the progress of the poet's soul from the immediacy of grief to the tranquil acceptance of the human condition with its consoling hope of immortality.

The material and the mood of the sections vary so greatly that it was necessary to impose certain structural divisions to hold the work together. Tennyson organized the poem around three consecutive Christmases, marking a development from private, violent grief to a sense of universal human sorrow and consolation that is no longer merely personal. Continuity is maintained by repeated images and themes, as well as by the gradual enlargement of the poet's spirit through his experience of grief. Instead of logical exposition or philosophic detachment, the poet follows the vague, digressive, natural rhythms of human thought and emotion. There is a stream of impressions, dreams and intellectual concepts as they are worked upon by the imagination. These frequently break off, to be resumed again in another context and often on another level. They are interrupted by reminiscences and by changes of mood. The likeness of this pattern is strikingly similar to the actual confusion of human thought and feeling, and through it the poet successfully communicates a vivid picture of his unconscious mind working in union with conscious art. This takes place in an interplay which is ordered only by the unique personality which is the source of this thought and feeling. As in a diary or in the Joycean stream-of-consciousness technique used in the modern novel, Tennyson relies on a fundamentally psychological unity, which represents the reality of his emotion more accurately than could the classic, chronological narrative of events.

STRUCTURAL ANALYSIS

Proem

These eleven introductory **stanzas** were composed in 1849. In them, the poet speaks in an objective tone, commenting on the awful majesty of God and the fragility of man. The contrast between man and God explains our inability to account for the mysteries of existence except by blind faith. Despite our lack of certainty, we have intuitions of God's involvement in the world because He created it, and we must hope that our knowledge of Him will grow with our own moral and spiritual progress. The poet asks forgiveness for his grief and doubt, aware that merit in the sight of man does not guarantee any merit in the eyes of God.

Part I (Sections 1-27)

Though the experience of suffering is necessary for the soul's advance in wisdom, it is impossible to be sure any future state of joy can match that which the poet enjoyed with his dead friend. The old yew tree under which the dead man lies embraces him physically; and the poet, watching, feels as though he were one with the insensible, vegetable nature which possesses his friend. Though nature will awake in this world again, men once dead will not return. The meaninglessness of nature and the suffering she inflicts on man cause the poet to doubt a beneficent order in the universe; and he debates whether to accept this doubt as the ultimate answer, or to "crush" it with faith. His will must battle the impulse to drift numbly in his sense of overwhelming loss. Writing gives direction and purpose to his sorrow, though by it he runs the risk of cheapening his feelings, to which he can never do justice in mere words. He dwells upon the **irony** of the unsuspecting, waiting friend or lover, thinking of the beloved, all unaware that at this very moment the loved one has ceased to exist. Standing before Hallam's house on Wimpole Street in London, the unhappy poet drives the knowledge in upon his benumbed spirit that his friend is forever gone; yet he cannot help noticing that "The noise of life begins again," and that the "blank day" has once again broken through the night. The poetry he writes, loved by Hallam, is planted like a flower on his tomb, and may wither there or not, for all the poet cares.

He relives the bleak days when the ship bearing Arthur's body travelled from Trieste to England. Like the calm sea, the calm autumn landscape, and the still heart of the dead man, the poet's soul is possessed by "calm despair." Like the dove leaving Noah's ark, his spirit goes over the water in search of his friend. He has not fully plumbed the depths of his loss; if the ship were to come and Hallam's body be borne off onto the land, the poet would not be surprised to see his friend come toward him whole, and in the flesh. The violence of an autumn storm makes him fancy that Hallam is at rest and knows nothing, but the rising wind suggests to him the ascent to a heavenly realm which he trusts Hallam has made. It surprises him to realize that one man can feel both violent emotion and calm despair, just as autumn is both stormy and still. Underneath the changes, his soul may be stunned and lifeless, he feels, like a lake which merely reflects life but does not participate in it.

As Hallam is buried, the poet would like to give him his own breath of life, but has the poor consolation that Hallam's body is mingling with England's earth. Like the river's rise and fall, the poet's deepest grief is periodically silent, then overflows in words. Like the shepherd in the standard pastoral **elegy**, the poet thinks of his songs as blown upon the pipes which are made from the grasses of Hallam's grave. Others mock him, saying that the social and scientific upheavals of his day make such private grief selfish; but the poet goes on with his song because instinct compels him. The memory of the close friendship with Hallam as they went through the inevitable seasons of four years together reminds the poet that the same "shadow" of death awaits him also. In their happy, unsuspecting youth, they moved by intuition and the pleasures of Greek philosophy, but even this was not perfect bliss. Even the sun has sunspots, and the past seems more beautiful than it is because of its distance from us in our present grief. Burdens seemed lighter then, because they were shared by his friend.

The poet intends to struggle on with his writing, as proof that time cannot change the quality of love. He would rather die, if the all-knowing God sees in his future a cooling of his love for Hallam. Both beasts and unfeeling men may not suffer as he does, but the poet feels that his divided, unhappy and confused condition is superior to that of one who has never "loved and lost."

Part II (Sections 28-77)

The first Christmas after Hallam's death is near, but the poet feels only sorrow that his friend does not celebrate it with him. Though he almost wishes he were dead himself, he cannot help being affected by the church bells, which had always meant for him Christmas joy in boyhood. In the shadow of death, in dismal, rainy weather, the family makes a pretence at celebration. They sing on Christmas Eve, and are consoled. Their faith tells them that the dead do not dwell apart from their living friends, and that the change of death is not so great as it appears. The renewal of the world at the birth of Christ, and the birth of day out of night, remind the poet that God has given us hope of immortality. When Mary rejoiced in the return of Lazarus from the dead, she knew well enough to turn her eyes to Christ, who was the source of that life enjoyed by her brother.

Those whose lives are dominated by faith, prayer and good works should never be scorned by those who feel that they are above simple faith and live only by reason. It is easier for the latter to stumble into sin. Without immortality, the poet declares, there is no meaning to life. Without God, the order of the universe would be impossible, and love would be no more than mere physical lust. We know heavenly truth through intuition and experience. Christ taught us truth in the lesson of his life, and even savages can read from this simple textbook. Urania, used by Milton in *Paradise Lost* as the Muse of Heavenly Poetry, argues that the poet should not treat such matters in his profane poetry; but Melpomene, the Muse of **Elegy**, answers for the poet that human hearts are comforted by earthly songs, especially when heavenly truths are hinted at in those songs.

Despite the coming of spring and the slight solace from his poetry, the poet continues to mourn. He finds a kinship with the old yew tree over Hallam's grave, which sheds its cloud of pollen and then droops darkly in decline. All temporal things must endure change; the poet is not alone. When the bride leaves her parents' home, she returns from time to time, bringing new and different joys to them. Hallam, unlike the bride, does not return to his friend to share his new knowledge and life. The poet wishes vainly to follow his friend, but is afraid that he will forever be far behind Hallam in the latter's race to God. If, however, the soul sleeps between death and universal resurrection, they will wake together on the same level, as though they had never been separated. If the dead drink the water of oblivion, then they do not grow continuously in personality and knowledge, yet they may retain some hint of the past in the dim recesses of their minds. Tennyson hopes that should Hallam experience such a memory, he will be reminded by Tennyson's angel of his old friend who mourns for him. The purpose of our bodies is to help us develop a sense of separateness from other persons, and this advance in personality carries over into the development of the mind. The dead must remember the past or not be themselves, and when he and Hallam remember their "rich landscape" during the eternity before them, the five years of their friendship will be the richest. There must be at least a moment after death when souls know each other as distinct personalities, even if afterwards they are merged in one God and know no more.

The poet reminds us that he does not intend, in his scattered verses, to promote an entire analytical philosophy. Without intending profundity or completeness, he merely aims to transmute his brief doubts into songs of love. Underneath, his sorrow still absorbs the depths of his soul. Even though he can never love perfectly and the dead man will know his secret flaws, the poet begs his friend to be with him in life and death, knowing that he will see the sins of men on earth with the sympathetic eyes of God. Though men have the sinless example of Christ before them, they continue to sin. Faith urges us to hope that nothing in nature or man is in vain, though it seems wrong to our eyes. The carelessness of nature, however, makes the poet doubt, and weakens his already faint hopes of immortality. Whole species are extinct, yet man with his dreams of goodness and beauty would be a mockery if he were like the rest of the animals. Our answer lies "behind the veil," and we can grasp it only with faith.

The poet recognizes that his songs are merely of the earth, and that he must leave off standing at the open grave. Yet he begs sorrow to be a companion to him even though he might superficially rejoice over trifles for a time. He wonders if Hallam, joyful in heaven, looks back to his dimly conceived past life and sees his old friend as an inferior being. Though this may be the case, he comforts himself that Hallam may be like a poor man who has become rich and influential; in his wealth, he may look back nostalgically on the simple life of his boyhood. In any case, Hallam can do with his friend whatever he wills. A happy thought strikes him, like a butterfly painfully struggling from its chrysalis: love itself cannot die, whether or not the dead friend remembers his companion. The poet himself does not forget his loss, though some may note that he takes pleasure in the world; it is only because he has learned kindness and sympathy from his suffering.

The poet dreams, and when his mind and will are stilled in sleep, Hallam lives for him again. In another dream, the poet wanders crowned with thorns to show his suffering. Some laugh at him, but an angel offers him consolation which he does not fully understand. When he thinks of Hallam now, his friend's face is vague, but in sleep his image rises again. He dreams of a trip to France the two friends took in 1830. On a stormy day, the poet notes with renewed grief the first anniversary of Hallam's death. No longer can he blame death or nature for the loss of Hallam, for he has seen that both operate according to immutable laws. Writing in the tradition of the pastoral **elegy**, he meditates on the fame that would have belonged to the dead man. Arthur Hallam's power has been turned inward to develop the riches of his soul, instead of outward, toward developing a reputation in the eyes of men. Hallam's soul beautifies even death itself, and the poet leaves his greatness to the imagination since he cannot describe it fairly. In this world, only accomplishment is noted, but in the next, Hallam's recognition will be based on his real worth. There is little the poet can do to increase his friend's reputation, for words will die with the race of men who speak them. If we look at past and present in proper perspective, they vanish into the distance with time and cease to exist for us, however real they were to men once. The poet does not care to what use his words will be put; he writes out of love and not for fame.

Part III (Sections 78-104)

The second Christmas since Hallam's death was celebrated "calmly." There was no storm outside, but only a "quiet sense of something lost." The family plays games, but this does not mean they do not grieve within themselves. Addressing one of his brothers, the poet declares that his love for Hallam was for someone greater than himself, not the same as his blood brother, who was an equal and raised to be like the poet himself. Had he himself died before Hallam, the latter would have borne the grief nobly, remained at peace, and made the loss into spiritual gain. The poet is disturbed to think that with time he might have loved Hallam more, but comforted by the realization that the grain of love was ripened in the instant of death's frost, instead of in its usual season. He does not object to the death of the body, for it is necessary during the progressive evolution of the soul from the physical to the divine plane. Still, he cannot reconcile himself to the loss of Hallam's physical presence.

As he contemplates the lateness of the spring's coming, this poet laments that the marriage of Hallam to Emily Tennyson had been prevented by tragedy. The two friends might have rejoiced in their children together, grown old in common work and accomplishment, and finally died united with Christ in one spirit. These dreams bring back his grief in all immediacy, and destroy his hard-won peace.

In Section 85 the poet addresses Edmund Lushington, who is to marry his youngest sister, Cecilia, and summarizes the progress of his soul to the present point. He desires other friends and he still wants nothing but the beloved's return. He imagines first Hallam's springtime return in bodily form, but then conceives a summer vision of Hallam appearing in his immortal form. Even if he should appear and prove himself by knowledge of the past, present and prophecies of the future, it would be impossible to see and recognize him. Only a spirit can commune with the dead, for only a spirit is totally at peace. Hungry for his friend, the poet sits alone in the summer night, rereading Hallam's letters. In a brief ecstasy of communion, the poet feels his soul mingle with that of Hallam, outside the natural dimensions of this world.

The poet defends his own and Hallam's modest confrontation of doubt as a higher form of religion than that of simple, smug believers who have never been intellectually honest with themselves. He thinks of his own spirit as a meek wife to the great and gifted spirit of Hallam. In section 98, he speaks to his brother Charles, who is about to take a trip with his bride. They will visit Vienna, where Hallam died. The poet is indifferent to the beauties of Vienna, though Hallam admired it, for it only reminds him of death's cruelty.

Section 99 marks the second anniversary of Hallam's death. The signs of autumn, despite their beauty, remind him of the solidarity in grief he experiences with all those who mourn at this season. Yet he notes, too, that many rejoice at this time, in contrast to his own mood; and nature is ambivalent in its mirror to man's feelings. He mourns the loss of the familiar scenes of Somersby, which remind him both of Hallam, who loved these scenes also, and of the joys he experienced there in his childhood. On the last night at Somersby, the poet dreams of his friend: he dwelled with the muses, who sang beautiful songs to a veiled statue of Hallam. A dove brought him a message from the sea, and the poet leaves his hall in a boat. He progresses along a river of time, leaving the hall and the past behind. As they travelled, the muses of his poetry accompanying him grew in strength and glory, like evolving mankind. At last, in a shining ship, Hallam greeted them and took his friend in his arms. But now Hallam was three times the size of an ordinary man. The maidens bewailed the loss of their poet, but Hallam insisted that they accompany himself and the poet to their final destination, a "crimson cloud," that lay like land upon the sea.

PART IV (SECTIONS 104-131)

The third Christmas celebration takes place in Tennyson's new home in Epping Forest. The location is new, without memories, and the mood of the poet is therefore calm and untroubled. Celebration, however, is not called for because all traditions must remain in the place and circumstance from which they came. The poet begs the Christmas bells to "ring out" grief, social wrongs, and his own long period of elegiac poetry. He desires a new age, wherein men will be nobler and happier, and where the confusion of creeds will cease in favor of a fuller, broader Christianity. Though the dead man's birthday is a day of bleak, howling winds, the poet celebrates it cheerfully, as if Hallam were present. The poet realizes that mourning will cut him off from the rest of humanity, and that he must seek wisdom among the living, not the dead. He recalls Hallam's virtues, and defends his own lukewarmness toward other, lesser men on the basis that having once known Hallam, others cannot thrill him. Tennyson imagines the great man that Hallam would have been had he lived, and wishes the world followed Hallam's pattern of growth in divine wisdom as well as mere worldly knowledge.

Spring brings rebirth to the poet's hopes, and even his grief is productive, looking forward to future reunion instead of backward to tragedy. The passage of time, which worked the creation of earth and the development of man, will increase his gift to Hallam when the two are reunited, for suffering produces moral and spiritual advance in the human soul. Each man must effect this by seeking to rise above the beast in his own nature. He will not accept the judgment of science that man is a mortal animal only. Love dominates both his past and his present, just as Venus, the planet of love, is both the morning and the evening star. Despite the appearance of change which marks all earthly things, and despite the terrible doubts in men's hearts over the mystery of an unknowable God, the poet chooses to believe. His faith is not based on rational proofs, but on the experience of God's fatherly love. Whatever the **catastrophes** in the socio-political realms of the day, faithful spirits apprehend the love of

God behind it all. In the coming age, kings and beggars will have no place; the ideal man of the future will be like Hallam.

Despite the reverses and the apparent futility of so many human activities, the poet sees that time carries human destiny toward a definite end. In that divine consummation of nature, humanity and God, there is present the soul of his friend and the highest aspects of their friendship. In loving his friend, the poet loves God and nature also; for him, Hallam has mingled his essence with all that is permanent and good in life. Though all else in man seems to falter, his free will stands firm, anchored in Christ, the living rock, and in his faith in what "never can be proved" until the vision of God which man receives in death.

As the poet celebrates the wedding of his sister, he acknowledges that he loves Hallam even more than he had before, but that his songs must no longer be sad. New life is infused into them by the present joyful circumstances. After the wedding, nature is asked to bless the couple. The soul of a child, later to be born to Cecilia, is imagined as it comes from heaven and begins to go through the stages of development from animal to human. In that child, as in all mankind, progress toward the ideal and toward God is recognized as human destiny.

Comment

In the Proem, or eleven introductory stanzas to "In Memoriam," the poet establishes the themes which are to dominate the poem as a whole. We see initially a God apprehended by faith, whom we understand first as creator and then as the source of spiritual sustenance in the individual's life and death. The emphasis is thus "incarnationalist," or upon God at work in the world of men. The poet never allows the concept of God-at-work to obscure the mystery of God-the-transcendent, above and beyond His finite creatures. That both aspects of God must be fused in our minds to approximate the overwhelming reality which is God Himself, is one of the major themes of the poem. The integrity, or wholeness of man, is similar to the oneness of God in His transcendental and immanent (incarnational) aspects. Man is confronted by a problem in dualism: death separates the soul and body, yet religion tells us that for Christian sanctity man must somehow unite soul and body in a reconciled whole.

The Proem states as one goal of man that "mind and soul, according as well, / May make one music as before," so that intellect and spirit must unite as well as spirit and body. There must be awareness of the absolute continuity of human existence, whatever plane each man's existence may be on. Man begins at the animal level of the senses, and progresses to the levels of mind and soul, and finally to the level of spirit; there is no break in his development, and this continuity provides the purpose and justification for his existence.

The levels of being are conceived in the Platonic sense; man develops from the animal to the spiritual by enlarging his consciousness until it merges with the infinity of God and he sees creation with the eye of divine vision. As there are levels in the development of the individual on his path to God, so there are levels of consciousness within the individual soul at any given time during its development. The poet declares in Section 52 that intellect and language only function on "the topmost froth of thought," that is, that emotional or subconscious depths exist beneath this surface which man is only faintly mindful of, and which the poet can suggest only by inference. Dreams, and one state of mystical trance during which he feels he has communed with the soul of the dead Hallam, mark the poet's excursion into these formless depths of soul which are unreachable in philosophical or theological terms.

The incomprehensibility of God, His nature and His ways with man, form the chief motif of "In Memoriam." Tennyson develops this theme through continuously repeated images, primarily through images of change. The flux which apparently dominates creation produces a doubt that any eternal stability can exist. Images of seasonal change and changes of place, direction and motion contrast with images of stability like the stars, especially the sun.

Seasonal changes form one of the chief structural and conceptual bases of the poem. Autumn ordinarily represents death and loss. The face of autumn is Janus-like: its storms and winds signify the shifting moods of suffering and doubt common to man, while its stillness signifies the calm of human despair. Always, the changes of season suggest the surface motion of the soul in emotional flux, beneath which is an abiding sorrow. Winter brings Christmas and therefore it is a promise of divinity and immortality, though it appears bleak and dead. New life is born in the spring, and spring represents the call to new human commitments. These are fulfilled in summer, which is a time of mystical communion with Hallam and a conviction of man's immortality and ultimate significance.

The mystery of nature and of human life produce the phenomena of faith and doubt. Doubt cannot be avoided if man looks critically and honestly at his situation, particularly at the suffering and death that condition all human experience in this world. Doubt itself is not evil, and can even promote a higher spiritual understanding, for it is a kind of suffering natural to mortal man. Suffering and death purify man and make him wise, and it is through this wisdom that man transcends the baser aspects of his nature.

This baser self is represented by the frequent beast image, while the spiritual desire of man is represented commonly by the bird or by song. The relationship between man and God is often symbolized by light, since light seems to partake both of the physical and the spiritual simultaneously. Song, birds and light also represent the virtue of faith, which is another, more positive and fruitful approach to the incomprehensibility of God and life. Faith is the intuitive response as opposed to the intellectual, merely rational response of the scientist. All aspects of the human soul must participate in man's response to his human predicament, and one alternately doubts or believes as his experience leads him toward the final vision of reality after death, which alone can perfectly resolve the conflict between faith and reason.

The suffering and death that mark human life have other uses. As man suffers, he grows in spiritual and moral stature. He becomes capable of larger human sympathies, and grows in patience and wisdom. Divine wisdom, as expressed in faith and in charity, takes precedence over mere human knowledge. These larger human sympathies are often symbolized by bells, particularly marriage bells and Christmas bells. As faith is one religious solution for the problem of suffering and death, so is charity another. Human love transcends time, death and change. The spiritual progress which it marks is part of the ripening universe, progressing toward a final, divine consummation, in which men will be perfected in preparation for their union with God.

Images of motion, indicating the development of man and nature, are prevalent throughout the poem. The most common image of motion (in the sense of change of direction and place) is that of the journey. The poet frequently refers to "paths" and "footsteps" as well as to the sea and travel by ship. These ordinarily refer to the plodding, struggling human being making his way painfully through the experiences of life and death. When the wind rises or birds take flight, on the other hand, man is making the more rapid, joyful spiritual ascent that requires another kind of motion than that of the "path." During the progress toward eventual union of living and dead in God, mankind develops from the level of the beast to that of super-personality. Beginning with the mere physical body, man's growth is more and more toward the unique and the personal. Our ultimate level will be that of supreme personality and eternal life, and these conditions answer the questing soul's doubts about the meaning of life and death.

Modern critical objections to "In Memoriam" have often centered on the poet's choice of immortality as a theme worthy of his most serious and exalted imaginative energies, at a time in history when religious answers to life's problems seemed less relevant than scientific answers. It has been held against Tennyson that he took personal survival after death so to heart, and critics have intimated that this concern is the mark of an insecure, ignoble or egotistical temperament. Actually, Tennyson saw immortality as the most dramatic illustration of the great debate between faith and doubt in the modern mind.

The immortality issue is the personal aspect of the crucial human problem: what is the nature of man? Either man is holy and immortal, with a spirit which transcends the merely animal, or he is simply an intelligent beast. The investigation of this essential problem, which has always engaged the philosophical, theological and poetic energies of men throughout the ages, is surely not without meaning or purpose for modern man. Critics are once again, since the decline of the first great burst of feeling against Tennyson's literary supremacy in the Victorian period, seriously aware of his insight into the universal human situation.

ESSAY QUESTIONS AND ANSWERS

Question: What is the role of reason in the life of man?

Answer: Despite the impact of science on modern man, Tennyson holds firmly to the belief that the whole man, with his will, intellect and emotions, must be considered as a unit. Reason alone cannot comprehend God. The philosophical and theological systems, explanations and proofs of God "are but broken lights" of God Himself. Tennyson defends the utter transcendence and mystery of God as he does the spirituality and immortality of man. We cannot know the whole of God with our reason, nor is reason sufficient to comprehend the nature of the whole man. Knowledge of creation is good, nevertheless, and it must "mix with men and prosper." The ultimate concerns of man cannot be tested by reason alone, however, only by reason under the tutelage of love and faith. Since logic is insufficient to discover **metaphysical** truth, we must come, in the end, to a faith which relies on the ideals and the love inherent in the human heart.

Question: How does the poet's vision of Hallam change throughout the poem?

Answer: In the first bitterness of grief, Tennyson feels that Hallam is mingled thoroughly and inextricably with physical nature, and that his presence is totally lost. The roots of the yew tree form a kind of prison for the body buried underneath. As the poet remembers the rich past he enjoyed with his friend, the conviction begins to grow that a soul so noble could not be obliterated without a trace. One of the chief concepts developed in the poem is that the ideals and aspirations in the best of men signify some higher source, purpose and end for the soul than mere extinction. Hallam's life and death serve as concrete evidence for this conviction. As the poet remembers the past, he sees Hallam as a very human flesh-and-blood companion, although superior to himself in natural endowments. This vision of his friend changes as the poet speculates further on the nature and purpose of man, on the life of the spirit and the destiny of the human race. Slowly, Hallam assumes the dimensions of the ideal, fully developed human end-product of the evolutionary process. He appears in the vision of the ship as a tall, shining figure of angelic power and wisdom, embodying the human soul in its final beatitude which is union, with God.

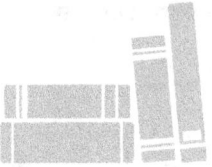

OTHER POEMS

ULYSSES AND TITHONUS

COMPOSITION

After Arthur Hallam's death, Tennyson retired to Somersby, where he spent much of the following year 1834. At times during this period, he would leave even Somersby for the small cottage by the sea at Mablethorpe, to mourn and write in solitude. "In Memoriam" was begun in this cottage and "Ulysses" was written there also. "Tithonus" was composed at the same time as "Ulysses," and is a complement to the more famous poem. It was not put into final form and published until 1860, though "Ulysses" appeared in the volume of 1842. Both poems are dramatic monologues, in unrhymed iambic pentameter.

By 1847, "Ulysses" was called by a reviewer one of the finest poems in English or any other language, and its reputation has persisted through the years. According to Tennyson's *Memoir*, it was a reading of "Ulysses" which prompted Sir Robert Peel to grant him his much needed pension of 200 pounds. Tennyson himself said about "Ulysses" that it reflected his own feelings soon after Hallam's death, particularly the belief that after tragedy, men must "go forward...braving the struggle of life." Twentieth century critics have complained that the tone of "Ulysses" is confused and does not suggest what Tennyson said he meant it to. According to them, restless Ulysses seeks escape from human obligations in favor of a Faustian search for knowledge beyond man's grasp. However, the magnificence of the language and the grandeur of the poem's mythic and philosophic associations have made the poem a general success with readers and critics alike.

SOURCES FOR ULYSSES

Ulysses (the Roman form of the Greek Odysseus) fought for ten years against the Trojans, and it was on his advice that the means for Troy's destruction was devised. He was represented as the wiliest and cleverest of the Greeks. Homer's *Iliad*, in which Ulysses first appears, is continued by the much later *Odyssey*, of which Ulysses is the hero. In the latter work, Ulysses' ten years of wandering and final regaining of his throne on the island of Ithaca are described. In the eleventh book of *The Odyssey*, when Ulysses is visiting in Hades, the seer Tiresias foretells that the hero must make a final journey with an oar over his shoulder, until he finds a land that does not know the sea or what his oar is. There he is to sacrifice to Poseidon (whom he had offended) and return to his home, to die a peaceful death surrounded by his people. *The Odyssey* ends with the hero's reunion with his wife and the re-establishment of his authority in Ithaca. There was a persistent legend throughout the Middle Ages about Ulysses and his last voyage, a legend that found its way into Canto 26 of Dante's *Inferno*. Tennyson evidently knew this passage well, for it is highly reminiscent of his own treatment of the hero. Some of the elements in Dante that re-appear in Tennyson's version are Ulysses' impatience of domestic obligations, his determination to gain knowledge hitherto unavailable to men, and his conviction that man was meant for a higher life than the merely social one. In the *Inferno*, unlike "Ulysses," the hero's ship comes to the end of the world and is sunk in a whirlpool. Tennyson considers his hero only at the dramatic moment of his quest's beginning.

SOURCES FOR TITHONUS

The tone of "Tithonus" is a more muted one, appropriate for the aged hero at the end of life. Like "Ulysses," it is a **dramatic monologue**, in which the hero of the Greek myth is given both personality and a wider symbolic significance than in the classical story. Eos (the Greek form of the Roman Aurora), goddess of dawn, loved the mortal Tithonus. Zeus granted her request to give Tithonus eternal life, but she did not think to ask for his eternal youth as well. As a result, Tithonus wasted into old age, but could not die, however much he wished to. At last, he was turned into a grasshopper, though Tennyson leaves out this ludicrous part of the legend in deference to the melancholy, philosophic tone of the poem. The atmosphere of "Tithonus" is similar to the sixteenth ode of the second book ("To Grosphus") of Horace's *Odes*, which Tennyson had known from childhood. The ode describes man's desire for tranquility, no matter how his ambition may militate against this ultimate good. Horace laments the restlessness of man, who can never escape himself, though he should travel far across the sea. Horace mentions that life is painless for no one; Achilles died young, Tithonus lived longer than he wished to. Death is a blessing, if only we regard it wisely. It is apparent that this Horatian insight forms a link between the restless Ulysses and the resigned Tithonus, who seeks only the peace of death.

PLOT ANALYSIS FOR ULYSSES

Ulysses, though king of Ithaca, is discontented. He soliloquizes on the dullness of his old age, spent with an old woman, a meekly dutiful son, and a rough and mindless people. He remembers that in his heroic past he lived life intensely, both in suffering and joy. Having travelled widely, he is wise in the ways of men, governments and ideas. For him, the value of life lies in the opportunity it offers for constant activity and inner growth. Ulysses cannot bear to think of wasting those few precious years he has left.

The narrative is here divided into a brief section which appears to mirror the thought of Ulysses as he says farewell to his son Telemachus, who will rule in his place. He commends his son's sense of duty, and his patience during the civilizing of his people. Yet Ulysses cannot embrace the ideals of Telemachus as his own, but comments, "He works his work, I mine."

Lines 44-70 form the third informal division of the poem. In this section, Ulysses is on board his vessel, waiting to set off on his last voyage. He meditates on the task before him, and on his old friends, the mariners who accompany him. Despite their presence, he is essentially alone, wrapped as he is in contemplation of his last great effort in life. It is necessary for him to close his life as gloriously as he spent it. "Men that strove with Gods" must not lose their ambition simply because they are old. As evening approaches, Ulysses tells his mariners that they may drown, but also suggests boldly that they may reach the Happy Isles, eternal dwelling place of those whom the gods wish to favor. Time may have diminished his strength, but it cannot change the nature of his "heroic heart," or strong will "To strive, to seek, to find, and not to yield."

Comment

The tone of the first section of "Ulysses" is personal, establishing both character and attitude. Ulysses' distress is not merely personal, however. He expresses weariness with all those things that root mankind in routine, domesticated lives, and this weariness has overtones of spiritual and intellectual discontent. At once Ulysses is established in our mind as one of the special souls not able to be satisfied with the simple pleasures of earthly life. He demands a high purpose and destiny regardless of the discomfort or disappointment which these may entail. Ulysses finds his island unbeautiful, with its "barren crags," his wife "aged," the laws he must rule by "unequal," and his people "savage." Thus, he rejects all goals embraced by most men: the natural and familiar beauties of one's homeland, love for one's wife, security in traditional law and order, and affection for one's people.

Ulysses is primarily interested in variety of experience rather than in stability or peace, as most men understand it. He declares, "I am a part of all that I have met," indicating that he has infused something of his own personality into every person and event that has touched his life. Therefore, he has indirectly won an immortality based on his wide-ranging experience in the world. Despite the fullness of his life in purely earthly, natural terms, Ulysses is not satisfied. His vision of life goes beyond the physical world, through which he always sees "that untravell'd world whose margin fades / For ever and for ever when I move." In his ambition and courage Ulysses intends to carry his search for fulfillment into realms beyond the material world, beyond merely human reason, into a transcendental, supernatural universe. He is consciously confronting death in his desire to know what is beyond this life. Instead of awaiting the inevitable conclusion of human life in fear or mere resignation, as does the ordinary run of humanity, Ulysses boldly approaches death in a spirit of martial adventure and intellectual curiosity. Presumably this approach, though non-Christian in inspiration, had meaning for the recently bereaved young Tennyson, struggling as he was with the various meanings of death for human beings.

In Ulysses' soliloquy on his son Telemachus, there is a noticeable change of tone. The scornful reference to his people as a "savage race" is muted to "a rugged people," and the old king is able to see a slow process of improvement as a distinct possibility for men. Some critics have felt that there is a note of condescension or sarcasm in Ulysses' attitude toward his son. It is true that Ulysses refers to Telemachus as a man of piety, meekness and "slow prudence," and that these qualities are totally counter to those that mark the young man's father. Yet Ulysses casts no aspersions on the usefulness of men like Telemachus; indeed he calls the young man "blameless." He is simply aware that not all men can fulfill themselves in terms of common social duties. Nor is it possible for all men to fulfill themselves by slow degrees, waiting for the evolutionary development of humanity in the future to see the final end of man. Some must strike out at once on uncharted seas, leaving security and human order behind them, without fear of disaster or death. There is a place for both types of men in this world, Ulysses realized.

The tone of the third section is a less violent, personal one than that of the other two sections. Instead of the sharp strokes of character delineation used previously, the poet in the third section widens the hero's vision so that he stands more broadly for all adventurous, unorthodox "Faustian" men. The time of the sailing has symbolic overtones also. Ulysses, like all men facing death, is in the twilight of his life, and plows ahead into the coming darkness. Tennyson himself was conscious of such a symbolic aspect to his own old age when he wrote the famous little poem "Crossing the Bar," in 1889. The seeking of life's last adventure is seen as a search for a "newer world," rather than for oblivion or mere quiescence. Tennyson here clearly sees, or desires to see, death as an active, creative and challenging human enterprise, one which elevates man rather than diminishes him.

PLOT ANALYSIS FOR TITHONUS

Tithonus addresses his immortal wife, Eos, in a **dramatic monologue** on his pathetic situation. While all nature repeats the cycle of life and death, he alone is different and withers in undesired immortality. Alone, he spends his life in the misty, eastern palace of the goddess of dawn, cut off from other human beings and their destiny.

He laments the loss of his youth, and recalls the days when he was chosen by the goddess as her mortal love. At that time, he seemed to himself as glorious as a god, and he therefore requested what was to be his later curse: immortality. Now he suffers bitterly from the contrast of his own old age and the goddess' perpetual youth. He cannot even find satisfaction in the tears Eos sheds for him in her pity. Tithonus wishes he had never aspired to a lot higher than that of other men. Death is not to be feared, but embraced, in solidarity with all humanity as one's necessary and proper fulfillment.

His memories of the past become even more immediate and vivid. Eos is once again vibrantly in love with him, and he enjoys the warmth of her love. He could not understand her and her love even then, for this mystic and supernatural union was beyond his merely human comprehension or appreciation. Now he is aware that the unequal union must be ended, and tells Eos, "my nature (can) no longer mix with thine," and that he is now cold and ready for death. He envies other men who are able to die, and begs his goddess to allow him to die also, and to mingle with the earth where he belongs.

Comment

Tithonus opens his discourse in a tone of impersonal melancholy, with reference to the general condition, not of man, but of all nature. The lines describing the inevitable decay for the woods are strongly reminiscent of the Horatian Ode which influenced Tennyson's poem. Only when Tithonus has mentioned the decay of nature, does he reflect on the life and death of man. From nature, Tithonus moves to man in general, and finally to himself in particular, because he is singular among men. This dramatic progression from general to particular contrasts with the strongly personal and almost egotistical tone of Ulysses. The latter, it will be recalled, progressed from self to the universal lot of man, the opposite of the pattern of Tithonus. "Tithonus" is clearly another approach to the problem of death, meant to complement the aggressive, defiant and restlessly seeking attitude of "Ulysses." Throughout "Tithonus", the tone is dreamy, plaintive and reminiscent. The hero looks back on life as a complete accomplishment, not as something to be added to, or to be given some ultimate purpose.

Tithonus sees himself as cut off from other human beings, isolated in the goddess' dwelling. Thus he deplores a condition actively sought and relished by Ulysses in the previous poem. The enemy of Tithonus is time, while that of Ulysses is the restriction placed on him by space and society. Ulysses deliberately seeks the unusual, while Tithonus desires only to fade into the common run of humanity. In his youth, Tithonus was rash enough to desire the singular favor of the gods, but now, in the wisdom of age, he repudiates the ambition that marked his youth and Ulysses' whole life.

In the last two stanzas of the poem, Tithonus hardly recognizes his old self, with its passions and delusions. While Ulysses' whole life was of a piece, that of Tithonus was broken by changes of attitude and character. He has lost the sense of his own continuity through time, and even his own identity. Such a man sees himself to be ready for rest and oblivion. To the sweetness of the goddess' love, he is now cold, with the coldness of death and indifference. Instead of desiring to keep the immortality and heavenly love he has been given, Tithonus wants only to share the common lot of man: returning to the earth and mingling with it as a sign of his final commitment to man and earth rather than to that "untravell'd world" longed for by the more adventurous Ulysses.

ESSAY QUESTIONS AND ANSWERS

Question: How do the central symbols in "Ulysses" contribute to the **theme** of human search and fulfillment?

Answer: As is common in Tennysonian **imagery**, the sea journey carries the major symbolic burden of Ulysses. The land is dull and safe, its crags are "barren," and there is no mystery in the hearth, a symbol of the home. At heart, Ulysses is a mariner, not a king. In Ithaca, on the land, he must perform the kingly function which is against his nature; but on the sea, he is simply another seeker. There he exposes himself to the mysterious power of the elements and to the unknown beyond the reaches of the land. In his great past as a hero, Ulysses was more mariner than king, more warrior than law-giver, more a traveller than a stable husband and father. The journey by sea allows him to live according to his nature, as the life on land does not, for it implies an embarking into the unknown and an abandonment of what has already been experienced and understood. Ulysses' desire for knowledge is several times symbolized by stars. He follows knowledge like a "sinking star," and intends to pursue his goal even past the sunset "and the baths of all the western stars," until death itself. The journey cannot begin until nightfall, which represents the abandonment of all those elements in life craved by the senses. The stars appear at nightfall, and signify for Ulysses the ultimate goals of human wisdom. They can be followed only in danger, darkness, and the despising of all creature comforts dear to other men.

Question: What would be the attitude of Tithonus toward those dreams of power and knowledge that motivate Ulysses?

Answer: The incomprehensible and supernatural love of the dawn goddess for Tithonus was repudiated by him as a goal for human life. Though the dim rapture they inspired in his youth is recalled with wonder and nostalgia, the same dream no longer interests the aged Tithonus. The dreams of youth are no longer suitable for old age, he feels, and even the remembrance of joy can ultimately be no solace to a man. Instead of a divine love and singular fate among men, Tithonus sees religion as the ultimate good, though not, of course, the Christian religion. The attitude toward death espoused by Tithonus is one of resignation, even relief. Death is the end of consciousness, and he has no hopes, such as Ulysses does, of adding further to personality and knowledge beyond the grave. The aims of Ulysses are thus repudiated one by one by Tithonus, who has gained from life what Ulysses desired and has seen it turn to ashes in his hand.

OTHER POEMS

LUCRETIUS

COMPOSITION

On his 1856 tour through Germany, with all its medieval relics, Tennyson was inspired to write not a romantic, but a classical poem. He was not a purely romantic poet like those of the early nineteenth century, but a neo-romantic, blending romantic and classical **themes** and styles. His early reading of the classics gave him a sense of familiarity with classical themes, and the subject of the Roman Lucretius allowed him to deal with the idea of materialism versus religion, a problem which he considered fundamental to the predicament of his age. Algernon Swinburne's (1837-1909) sensuous *Poems and* **Ballads** was published two years in advance of "Lucretius," and some critics believe Tennyson was encouraged by the work of the younger poet to experiment with a bold use of erotic material.

The poem was written in October, 1856, and published in *Macmillan's Magazine*, May, 1868. Public and critics received it well and many regarded it as a faithful restatement of the Roman poet's own beliefs and style. However, Lucretius did not express doubt as to the role of the gods in the life of men; this addition is Tennyson's own, and was doubtless included because he felt it was relevant to the situation of modern man.

BACKGROUND

Lucretius was a Roman poet who published his chief work, *De Rerum Natura* (*On the Nature of Things*) about 55 B.C. He was a disciple of the Greek philosopher Epicurus (342?-270 B.C.), who held that the universe was made up of eternal atoms, had no purpose and was ruled by no gods. Like Epicurus, Lucretius believed that a serene life of reason and enlightened self-gratification was the proper goal of each man, and that the gods and their demands should be eliminated from human consideration. Unlike Virgil (70-19 B.C.), whom Tennyson son admired, Lucretius embraced a code of non-involvement in society and the needs of other human beings. Virgil, like Tennyson, advocated a sense of responsibility to God and man as a proper human commitment, upholding the virtue of faith against the Lucretian code of futility. While Tennyson himself had felt the storm of doubt which forms the central crisis of his hero, he did not invest his poem with the inspiration of personal experience and spontaneous emotion. The effects are calculated, and critics have not failed to remark on the poet's lack of success in firing the reader's imagination or emotions. "Lucretius" is generally judged to be a fine showpiece with admirable technique and a genuinely classical atmosphere, but without the spark of lyric genius that would have raised it to the level of the poet's best work.

PLOT ANALYSIS

Lucretius' wife, Lucilia, feared she had a rival. Her husband, though loving her well enough, was concerned only with the life of the mind. She had a witch brew her a love potion, which caused Lucretius to go mad from the conflict between his sensual desires and his ideal of rational serenity.

He waked after a storm, and, in some agitation, recalled his dreams. First he remembered a vision of his own philosophic universe: atoms clashed purposelessly, creating and destroying, indifferent to man. Then he dreamed of the dissolute dictator Sulla, whose excesses caused civil war and rains of blood on Rome. From the earth, prostitutes sprang up instead of the warriors Lucretius expected, according to the myth of Cadmus. The prostitutes surrounded the dreamer, and closed in upon him. Next, Lucretius dreamed of the breasts of Helen of Troy, threatened impotently by the sword which cannot prevent her destruction of Troy. He reeled, "scorched" by the flames from Helen's breasts.

Lucretius wondered if he had offended the goddess of love by his refusal to sacrifice to her. Recalling that he honored her as the life-force in the introduction to his masterpiece, Lucretius declared that his tribute to her would outlast any recognition of her divinity by men. He begged Venus to coax Mars, the god of war, to cease drenching Rome in the blood of civil war. Then Lucretius speculated on the gods, remembering that his master Epicurus acknowledged them. The gods, if they exist, must live in a peaceful vacuum, totally removed from human or natural disturbances; yet he wondered how they could be eternal if they, like all things, were made up of atoms. He lamented that his faculties were numbed and that he could not realize his intention of guiding Memmius (to whom his great work was dedicated) to an understanding of the timeless gods.

After remarking upon the sufferings of man which were seen by the eye of the sun god daily, Lucretius began to examine the reasons for and against suicide. If one believed in the gods, one could, like Plato, justify refraining from suicide on the grounds that one had a duty to stay at the post assigned by the gods. But a man who believed that the gods cared nothing for men would be released from the obligation to serve them, and could remove himself from the world of human ills. Particularly distressing among these ills, Lucretius felt, was the triumph of flesh over intellect.

Lucretius recalled the myth in which Numa, Rome's legendary second king, forced two nature gods to reveal their secrets, much as Lucretius himself longed to do through the exercise of reason.

In his book, Lucretius had declared the existence of satyrs to be impossible, but now he had a vision of one chasing a naked nymph. The nymph, like Lucretius, was repelled by the lustful satyr, and turned to throw herself upon the dreamer. This repelled him further, though in his madness he no longer knew whether or not he wished to see what was going on behind the bushes where the nymph and the satyr had gone.

In childhood, Lucretius said, he had formed the habit of calling on the gods, and the habit came back to him, though he believed they did not care to hear him. He had once thought his life imitated their calm lack of feeling, but now he felt that a "monster" had overcome his will with "filthy hands." He compared himself to Lucretia, a Roman heroine who had killed herself after being raped. He, too, felt that self-inflicted death was an answer to dishonor. Lucretia's pride and honor gave birth to the strength of Rome, but like Rome, Lucretius was in the process of destruction.

Having decided what he would do, he invited nature to recombine the atoms of his body to form whatever she wished. His great poem would last until the dissolution of the world, he believed. In his search for peace, he felt that man must seize his goal however he might. He stabbed himself and his wife grieved over him. She declared she meant only to gain his affection, but he told her not to care whether or not she had failed in her duty, since man could not know where his duty lies.

Comment

The drama in "Lucretius" is centered on the progressive decay of a noble mind into madness. There are occasional intervals of lucidity, chiefly when Lucretius reaches into the past for incidents that sharpen the contrast of his pure and his fallen states. Throughout the poem, Lucretius remains in the twilight between madness and sanity, lust and intellectual integrity; and his confusion is intensified, in effect, by the serenity of the gods.

The dreams of Lucretius are all stormy, and reveal the rising, raging tide of madness beneath his superficial, slight hold on reality. A natural storm parallels the fury within Lucretius, during his mad night of dreams. In his dream of the atoms, Lucretius participates in the futile frenzy of creation and dissolution in the universe of his own devising. The second dream illustrates the overcoming of his own proud consciousness by the forces of sensuality. They are represented as constricting powers, limiting the individual's powers of will and his breadth of vision. The third dream, in which Helen destroys Troy and burns the dreamer himself, reveals the inevitable end of one who inhabits the burning city of lust. Lucretius' reaction to the sight of Apollo, who represents the sun, is chaotic, and troubled by the conflict between human suffering and divine serenity. The sun, in Tennyson's poetry, is often a sign of spiritual and intellectual integrity or power. It is significant that the sun is of no help to Lucretius in resolving his dilemma, and that it is merely "blinding."

Even in his madness, Lucretius gives a larger dimension to his tragedy. He links himself and his decay to the death of Rome. The dissolution of his body into atoms is made parallel to the ultimate extinction of his masterpiece as well. In his work, Lucretius denied the torments of the afterlife, and he claims that the work itself delivers men from fear of hell. This removes the last inhibition against suicide, and Lucretius is then free to embrace the tranquility of the gods, which is, ironically, death and dissolution into nature. The fate of the unbelieving Lucretius reflects Tennyson's own feeling that without religious faith, men degenerate into monsters.

ESSAY QUESTIONS AND ANSWERS

Question: Was Lucretius undone merely by a love philtre? Explain.

Answer: The chief sin of Lucretius was his divorce of mind from reality, and self from society. His philosophy has the same basic flaw. Man must tend to his own selfish needs, Lucretius feels, without consideration of higher obligations. That Lucretius lived this creed diligently cannot be doubted. In his desire for a self-contained, untroubled existence, he ignored the needs of his wife and this drove her to obtaining the philtre. The neglect of his human ties and the duties they entailed was responsible for the fatal drink which in turn brought about Lucretius' downfall.

A second cause of Lucretius' fall from intellectual grace was the unacknowledged furor churning in his unconscious mind. Through his dreams, Lucretius learned that he was not free of the common brutish heritage of man, as he had supposed he was. The beast lurked in him, as in all men, and this realization convinced Lucretius that the intellectual foundation upon which he had hoped to build his life was a mockery. Unlike the great active heroes of mythology, Lucretius refused to face his own monster honestly, and slay him in open battle.

Question: What images does Tennyson use to convey the instinctual life of "the beast" as opposed to the pure life of the mind?

Answer: The calm eye of the sun, or spiritual faculty of man, is obscured throughout the poem by storms of passion. Lightning strikes the hollow mountain, releasing the waters of the earth, a pattern of images vividly suggestive of the erotic dance which is soon to follow. In his conscious state, the dreamer resists the meaning of these images, for he is committed to a complete separation of mind and matter, spirit and flesh. Besides images of lust, the dreamer is also overcome by images of blood and fire, here signifying brutal discord between man and man, with the resulting destruction of both Troy and Rome. Lust and the urge for power are the chained beasts that are released when man attempts to live by reason alone. Reason is too frail to hold the emotions in check without the acknowledgement of the gods and the sense of duty which this acknowledgement entails.

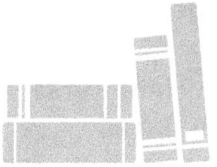

OTHER POEMS

DEMETER AND PERSEPHONE

COMPOSITION

As Tennyson approached his eightieth year, he was afflicted both by disease and by the loss of a son. He lived quietly at Aldworth, enduring his gout and failing eyesight, writing as much as his condition permitted. His son, Hallam, asked him to write a poem on Demeter because he was aware that Tennyson thought her "one of the most beautiful types of womanhood." Tennyson, as usual, did not write the poem as an exercise in the classical style, but insisted on giving it relevance to modern man. Both father and son were still grieving over the unexpected death of the younger son, Lionel. Lord Dufferin had invited the young man to India, and there he had fallen ill of a jungle fever, which killed him on his sea voyage home (1886). Lionel had been a gifted writer and charming young man, married only eight years when he died, and he left three young sons behind. Tennyson felt keenly the waste of talent this death involved. It may be that "Demeter" was an artistic vision of his grief for his own lost child, just as "In Memoriam" reflected his loss of Hallam. The preface of *Demeter and Other Poems* was dedicated to the Marquis of Dufferin, in commemoration of Lionel's death. The poem itself, a

dramatic monologue in **blank verse**, was the chief poem of an entire volume, published in 1889. The *Memoir* suggests that it was written several years earlier, in 1887, shortly after Lionel's death, and before the serious illness that threatened Tennyson's life in 1888.

SOURCES

The Homeric Hymn to Demeter is the source of the legend of Demeter, goddess of agriculture and of the fruitful earth. It was she who brought man grain, as Prometheus gave him fire. Her daughter by Zeus, Persephone, represented the grain itself, which spends part of the year in the dark earth and part of the year ripening in the sunshine.

Hades, god of death, carried off Persephone as his bride, as she was picking flowers in the valley of Enna in Sicily. Demeter, grieving, wandered over the earth in search of her daughter, and was too sorrowful to make the crops grow. Zeus at last granted her plea to restore Persephone to the land of the living. However, Persephone had eaten six pomegranate seeds while in the underworld, and this gave Hades a claim on her. Zeus decided to allow the girl to spend half the year with her mother and half with her husband. The myth accounts for the seasonal death and rebirth of vegetation. It was the basis for the Greek Eleusinian mysteries, which applied the rebirth of the vegetation concept to the regeneration of the human soul after death.

PLOT ANALYSIS

Demeter addressed her daughter, Persephone, describing her as she had just been brought by the god Hermes from the realm of the dead. The girl had been brought to Eleusis, a Greek city which was later the site for the Greek mysteries in honor of Demeter. Demeter recalled the awakening of her daughter to the reality of life again, after her death - like sleep. The appearance of the sun completed the rebirth, and mother and daughter embraced in its light. Demeter marvelled at her daughter's superior nature, which has now known both death and resurrection, all due to her mother's "mighty...childless cry."

Once more in Enna, Persephone's presence brought the flowers into bloom, and they carpeted the meadows, except for the dark, gravelike "blur of earth" left by the chariot of the king of the dead when he had abducted Persephone. This reminded Demeter that her happiness was at the mercy of Hades' return for his wife. She was relieved to see that even that dark earth flowered when Persephone's foot touched it.

Demeter told Persephone how she had grieved when the girl had first been abducted. She envied mortal mothers, but did not hesitate to nurse their sick babies on her travels around the world looking for her own lost child. Even while the happy mothers awoke to find their sick children well, Demeter had gone off into the night, bewailing the loss of Persephone. Demeter begged the winds, the seas, all of nature, to tell her the whereabouts of her child, but they could not. As she travelled the earth, she sorrowed for humanity as well as for herself, because she saw everywhere relics of man's weakness and mortality. Even the Fates, who spin the destinies of mortal men could not tell where the daughter of a goddess was to be found, but pointed to a higher Fate beyond themselves.

In a dream, Demeter saw the ghost of Persephone. The ghost told her that Zeus, "the Bright one," had promised his brother Aidoneus, "the Dark one" (Hades or Pluto), that the child of the earth mother was to belong to the God of Night, the Lord of the Dead. This revelation caused Demeter to curse the gods, who were remote from man, in heaven while she suffered on earth, just as suffering man endured trial. Human beings seemed to her more noble than the callous gods. All nature was drowned in her tears, and "helpless man" was afflicted by the loss of his crops.

Zeus, noticing the failure of men to honor him with their sacrifices because of their troubles, decreed that Persephone was to stay nine months with her mother and three months in the realm of the dead with her husband. Demeter now planned that she would once again bless the fields. But she was bitter against the Olympians, and believed that the Fates foretold the advent of new and gentler gods when they referred to a Fate beyond themselves. She envisioned gods who would help man rather than harm him, at last converting even Hades itself into heaven. At such a time, Persephone could dwell always with her mother in sunshine, and be worshiped by men with love instead of fear. Men would be higher in the evolutionary scale than they were at present, and would no longer fear hell. The Stone of Sisyphus, which had to be pushed up hill eternally, only to fall back, would cease to be a fearful example to men, as would the Wheel which tormented Ixion in Hades. No longer would warriors walk silently on the Elysian fields among the asphodel (daffodils), the legendary flowers of Elysium, land of the heroic dead.

Comment

The poem begins with the dramatic retelling by Demeter of Persephone's change "from state to state." She compares Persephone with a migrating bird, falling exhausted in its homeland. Tennyson often uses the image of a bird to suggest flights of mind or soul, and he uses it here to mark the change of Persephone from death to rebirth. Tennyson also uses the inevitable cycle of the seasons to suggest the regeneration of the human soul, particularly in "In Memoriam." The myth of Persephone is basically a vegetation myth, mirroring the apparent death and rebirth of plants with the changing of the seasons. Thus, in Tennyson's thought, it is a suitable vehicle for a poetic discussion of immortality, his favorite subject.

After the experience of death, Persephone's memory must be restored. She must regain her "lost self;" the continuity of her existence and the integrity of her identity have been broken. The song of the nightingale and the light from the moon remove the likeness of death from Persephone that was due to her sojourn with Hades. It is not, however, until the appearance of the sun that Persephone fully regains her soul and is able to recognize and love her mother. For Tennyson, the sun has a revivifying function much like that of the Holy Spirit, and it is often a symbol in his poetry of the soul influenced by God. Persephone is described as one who has gone into the depths of death and returned, "lighted from above...by the Sun."

The entire third stanza is a panorama of contrasts. Light and dark, life and death, flowers and unflowered earth, and loving mother versus the dark husband from out of hell. Demeter contrasts Enna when Persephone was stolen away, with Enna when Persephone has returned. Flowers and sunlight represent the life-giving influence of Demeter, while the words "dark" and "midnight-maned" represent the stifling forces of decay and death.

Demeter also contrasts, in the fourth stanza, the bleakness of life when Persephone was lost, with the sunny joy brought back with her upon her return to earth. In her search for an answer to her suffering, Demeter penetrates into the depths and heights of nature. In doing so, she makes her grief universal, and involves herself with every man. The empty tombs and temples which she sees suggest a whole civilization without faith or purpose. She sees the hearth, center of family life, "shatter'd," the shaft or weapon of man broken, and "The scorpion crawling over naked skulls." There is no answer to her suffering in merely human terms, and she must do as the Fates tell her: look for a truth that transcends the visible.

As she puts the old gods behind her and achieves a deeper solidarity with the problems of the human race, Demeter sees man as nobler than those who cannot suffer. The remote gods on Olympus know nothing of love and death, though they have given their consent to Demeter's own suffering. Having shared the lot of man, Demeter knows man's needs as no Olympian can. She envisions, toward the end of the poem, a new race of gods. Tennyson's cycle of decay and regeneration comes into play here, as does his goal of relating the myth to modern life. He suggests that the gentler religion of Christianity, in which God suffers with and for man, will ultimately break down the barriers of death and darkness. Again he sees a race of men who exist on a higher plane than ours, a theme of the latter part of "In Memoriam." Since the essence of this new religion was to be love, there could be no place in it for hell. Instead of being Queen of Death, the daughter of the earth mother would become a Queen of Love. Her harvest would be not only grain, but eternal life, and love would be the universal worship given to her by man.

ESSAY QUESTION AND ANSWER

Question: How does Demeter's voice gradually become that of universal man in the poem?

Answer: As the goddess of agriculture, Demeter is a figure naturally appropriate for representing the source of man's life. She nourishes his body, and, by extension, his soul also. At first, the mother rejoices in an individual paradise, aware of nothing but her daughter's embrace. In the second stanza, she senses that her daughter has gained a higher knowledge, not available to the mother, because she, like man, both dies and lives again. Demeter refers to her own plea for Persephone's return as "the mother's childless cry," for she has now broadened her vision enough to see herself as the universal sorrowing mother. In the fourth **stanza**, she strengthens the link between herself and earthly mothers by declaring that she envies them their children, and even suckles those mortal children herself. The fourth **stanza** continues with the search of Demeter, which increasingly identifies her with the condition of suffering humanity. She herself comments on the link between them: she "grieved for man thro' all my grief" for Persephone. In the last **stanza** of the poem, her complaint against the Olympians gives her complete solidarity with modern, suffering, doubting humanity. She voices the universal objection of man to belief in gods who ordain his lot and callously leave him to suffer it alone. Looking toward an evolutionary improvement in religion and in the nature of man, Demeter speaks with the voice of the human prophet, promising a future in which man can be perfectly reconciled to God.

ALFRED TENNYSON

CONCLUSION

BACKGROUND OF THE VICTORIAN AGE

Those years of the nineteenth century in which Tennyson came of age and flourished as a poet were years of almost frantic change. The center of European power had shifted from Paris to London, and England was in the process of capturing the world's markets through trade and colonialism. Her booming population, which was deserting the country for the city, her rapidly industrializing cities, and her powerful navy, assured her of a leading position in the modern world. The early Victorian period (1832-48) was marked by political upheavals and domestic catastrophes. The common people, worn down by depression, famine and poverty, exploded in the Chartist agitation demanding the vote for the poor. The era was heavy with foreboding, for many feared a civil war like the one which had toppled the French monarchy at the end of the eighteenth century. Social protest literature abounded. From 1848 to 1870, there was a period of stability and prosperity. The new era of Free Trade (begun by the repeal of tariffs on foreign grain in 1846) had benefited the economy and the condition of the poor. It was a period of complacency about social conditions in which attention was turned to intellectual matters, especially the apparent conflicts between new scientific views and those of traditional Christianity. The reforming urge was transferred from the social to the religious area, and a moral earnestness affected writers of the entire period, whether they were believers or skeptics. The Oxford movement followed the line of renewed and deepened religious faith under men like John Henry Newman, while the secular-minded intellectuals tried to relate the new insights into evolution, geology and astronomy to man's place in the universe. During the Late Victorian period (1870-1901) the old stability was again in danger. Germany under Bismarck had risen to challenge England as a major power, as had the United States. The English depression of 1873-1874 cast doubt upon the success of Victorian economic achievements. Men of letters, retreating from the apparently insoluble problems of society, dwelled on the more ideal images of reality to be found in art, and on the aristocratic pleasures as understood by poets like Byron. Attitudes of the previous generation were satirized and "moral earnestness" fell out of fashion, though it had met the needs of English readers for over half a century.

EFFECTS OF THE VICTORIAN AGE ON TENNYSON

The literary pressures of his age weighed heavily upon Tennyson, and the results are evident in much of his work. Above all, the Victorians felt that poetry existed primarily to be useful, and not for its own sake. In the fact of violent social and intellectual upheavals, the Victorians wanted to contemplate the stability of the home, of the Christian faith, of moral virtues and of patriotic ideals. Their love for the homely and familiar often resulted in a poetry of sentimentality instead of imagination. A successful poet had to echo the optimism, hopefully embraced by his country, against the fears of civil war and the passing of the old rural-aristocratic order. Tennyson was suited on many of these counts to be the voice of the Victorian age. In writing domestic idylls, Tennyson was able to bring to his work an eye for accurate detail, the pictorial skill necessary to sketch real landscapes, a personal conviction that love was inevitably bound to marriage, and the desire to work with simple emotions and uncomplicated psychological types.

The crisis of religion, as it confronted the new science, absorbed Tennyson's mind as it did the mind of his age. Tennyson avoided mere doctrinal **exposition** in his poetry and dwelled on the more universal, subjective and intuitive aspects of religion. His interest lay in exploring the relation of doubt to faith, and the existence of the soul after death. These were dealt with in terms of man's inner life and spiritual experience, not in terms of an intellectual or logical system of theology. In his political views Tennyson was much less inclined than in his religious outlook to confront the new realities of the Victorian period. Like most of his contemporaries, Tennyson felt that reforms ought to proceed slowly, that trade, science and law would eventually help the lot of the poor, and that the great (the aristocrats) were destined to rule the common run of humanity. Finally, Tennyson was strongly influenced by the literary climate of his time. His period of early development had been at the end of the romantic period, when a reaction to the excesses of Byron had set in and a new emphasis on form and discipline was in force. This brought a return of classical devices and themes, in which Tennyson participated: and it resurrected Keats, the most formal of the romantic poets in the estimation of the critics. The writers Tennyson admired most were romantics: Coleridge, Poe and Whitman. It was not until the end of Tennyson's life that the pendulum began to swing back toward the Byronic in verse and the new French naturalism in prose.

TENNYSON'S STYLE

It has frequently been noted by scholars that Tennyson's style did not undergo an orderly, definable development. Aside from his most youthful poems, the variety in Tennyson's work was primarily in subject matter and the use of literary devices like the monologue, rather than in literary quality. After a period weak in productions of permanent value (1857-1880), Tennyson seemed to recapture his earlier genius. His language became more stately, rich in strong, simple, Anglo-Saxon words, and more heroic and objective in style. Throughout his work, certain stylistic elements can be traced. Especially in descriptive passages, there is a sustained pattern of soft vowels, with sibilants and gutterals avoided in favor of flowing, mellifluous sound. Perhaps from Virgil, whose *Aeneid* had greatly influenced him, Tennyson learned to use devices to capture sound: **alliteration**, repetition of words and particularly onomatopoeia (commonly of bird sounds). Less happy, perhaps, was his fondness for periphrasis, which marked his notably unsuccessful poems; the simplest of objects or events were disguised elaborately in rich, overdone descriptive phrases. Such devices have been largely responsible for the violent critical reaction against Tennyson after his death.

TENNYSON AND HIS CRITICS

While modern men often look upon Tennyson's work as hypocritical or schoolgirl-prim, his contemporaries sometimes expressed the opposite view. As late as the 1860's, some thought Tennyson an immoral poet, an opinion which they must have felt was confirmed by the more purple passages in "Lucretius," a poem that might have been influenced by the hotly romantic work of Swinburne. Critics have also accused

Tennyson of being overly simple and intellectually inferior. Yet some contemporaries felt him to be overly subtle and obscure, especially in the symbolism of *The Idylls of the King*. More widely accepted views of Tennyson's defects seem likely to stand the test of time, however. Except for "Maud" and "Lucretius," Tennyson's longer works reveal an inability to organize his material into a powerful structure; the works remain a series of disorganized inspirations, despite Tennyson's frequent attempts at revision. All that is best in Tennyson indicates that his specific genius lay in lyrical description, yet his age did not encourage the development of this gift. Instead, its pressures led him to represent in poetry the "real" world, often a world devoid of imagination. However, his frequent choice of classical themes enabled him to transcend the limitations of Victorian complacency and provincialism. With such **themes** he could combine objectivity and grandeur with rich description and a high moral vision. After the long period when Tennyson was almost worshipped by the public, it was perhaps inevitable that a younger literary generation should rebel against him as the idol of its fathers. This critical trend persisted well into the twentieth century, and its vehemence has consigned a large portion of Tennyson's more sugary or **didactic** works to oblivion. The twentieth century critic demands originality, spontaneity and absolute sincerity; he is suspicious of elaborate style, careful revision, and formalism. Some modern critics seem to feel that Tennyson can only be appreciated if we extract from his work all that is not particularly of interest to contemporary man. All that is specifically Victorian must be "erased". Less drastic measures are advocated by others, who are now able to view the Victorian age dispassionately. They would have us simply enjoy Tennyson's genius when it is apparent, and forgive him at moments when it is not, a procedure which is followed, after all, with the works of every other poet.

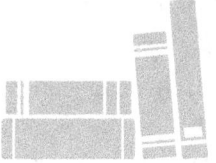

ALFRED TENNYSON

BIBLIOGRAPHY

PRIMARY SOURCES

Hallam, Arthur Henry, *The Writings of Arthur Hallam*, ed. T. H. Vail Motter, New York and London, 1943.

Tennyson, Alfred, *Poems by Two Brothers*, ed. Hallam Tennyson, London, 1893.

Tennyson, Alfred, *The Works*, 1 vol., Macmillan, 1913.

Tennyson, Alfred, *Works*, Eversley ed., 9 vols., London, 1907-8.

Tennyson, Hallam, *Alfred Lord Tennyson, A Memoir*, 2 vols., London and New York, 1897.

SECONDARY SOURCES

Biography

Benson, Arthur C., *Alfred Tennyson*, London, 1904.

Brooke, Stopford, *Tennyson: His Art and Relation to Modern Life*, London, 1894.

Lang, Andrew, *Alfred Tennyson*, Edinburgh and London, 1901.

Lounsbury, Thomas R., *The Life and Times of Tennyson*, New Haven, 1915.

Nicolson, Sir Harold, *Tennyson: Aspects of His Life, Character, and Poetry*, London, 1823.

Turnbull, Arthur, *Life and Writings of Alfred Lord Tennyson*, London and New York, 1915.

Waugh, Arthur, *Alfred Lord Tennyson*, London, 1892.

Criticism

Baum, Paull F., *Tennyson Sixty Years After*, Chapel Hill, 1948.

Bowden, Marjories, *Tennyson in France*, Manchester, 1930.

Bradley, A. C., *A Commentary on Tennyson's "In Memoriam,"* London, 1929.

Brookfield, Frances M., *The Cambridge "Apostles,"* London, 1906.

Chapman, E. R., *A Companion to "In Memoriam,"* London, 1888.

Critical Essays on the Poetry of Tennyson, ed. John Killham, New York, 1960.

Eidson, John, *Tennyson in America*, Athens, Georgia, 1943.

Gwynne, Stephen, *Tennyson: A Critical Study*, London, 1899.

Jones, Richard, *The Growth of the Idylls of the King*, Philadelphia, 1895.

Luce, Morton, *A Handbook to the Works of Alfred Lord Tennyson.*

Maccallum, M. W., *Tennyson's Idylls of the King*, New York, 1894.

Masterman, Charles, *Tennyson as a Religious Teacher*, 1900.

Mattes, Eleanor B., *"In Memoriam": The Way of the Soul*, New York, 1951.

Mustard, W. P., *Classical Echoes in Tennyson*, New York, 1904.

Paden, W. D., *Tennyson in Egypt*, Kansas, 1942.

Pyre, James, *The Formation of Tennyson's Style*, Madison, Wisconsin, 1921.

Shannon, Edgar, *Tennyson and the Reviewers*, Harvard, 1952.

Tennyson, Hallam, *Tennyson and His Friends*, London, 1911.

Articles

Basler, Roy P., "Tennyson the Psychologist," *South Atlantic Quarterly*, XLIII (1944).

Burton, Katherine, "Hallam's Review of Tennyson," *Modern Language Notes*, XLV (1930), 224-225.

Green, Joyce, "Tennyson's Development During the 'Ten Years' Silence' (1832-1842)," *PMLA*, LXVI (1951), 662-697.

Haight, Gordon S., "Tennyson's Merlin," *Studies in Philology*, XLIV (1947), 549-566.

Stevenson, Lionel, "The 'High-born Maiden' Symbol in Tennyson," *PMLA*, LXIII (1948), 234-243.

Wilner, Ortha L., "Tennyson and Lucretius," *The Classical Journal*, XXV (1930).

www.ingramcontent.com/pod-product-compliance
Lightning Source LLC
LaVergne TN
LVHW011708060526
838200LV00051B/2810